You're Worth It!

Pat Rinker

faith
CATHOLIC
books

Printed with ecclesiastical permission. Most Reverend Earl Boyea. August 3, 2012.

International Standard Book Number: 978-0-9854762-1-2
Cover and text design by Janna Stellwag
FAITH Catholic

Artwork by istockphoto.com

Distributed by FAITH Catholic, 1500 E. Saginaw Street, Lansing, MI 48906

Printed and bound in the United States of America.

ISBN: 978-0-9854762-1-2 (pbk)

You're Worth It!

Developing a daily walk with Jesus is one of the most essential practices for growing in discipleship. Pat Rinker, in "You're Worth It!" takes the difficulty out of daily prayer. Pat provides a practical, easy to follow plan and process that addresses relevant adolescent issues, and in the end, engages teens in the Scriptures, personal reflection and prayer. Young people need a guide in developing essential spiritual practices, and Pat has delivered a great one.

– Frank Mercadante, Executive Director, Cultivation Ministries

Young people often experience a disconnect between Scripture and everyday living. In this devotional, Pat Rinker helps young people INTENTIONALLY REFLECT so they can make sense of both "lectio divina" (the word of God) and CONNECTING it to "lectio vita" (the word of daily living). Pat's love of Scripture and young people show clearly as he offers stories, challenges, insights and journal opportunities/questions to help (young) disciples grow in their understanding and faith in Jesus. I'd recommend this to teens who want to get a better "grip" on Scripture and how it applies to daily living.

– Mike Patin, Catholic Speaker/Faith Horticulturist

You're Worth It!

Dedication

First and foremost, I dedicate this Scripture devotional for teens to God the Father, who loves us more than we can imagine. It is for Him that we live, and it is because of Him that we have our being.

And to Jesus Christ, who redeemed us. He never gives up on us. His words, "Father forgive them for they know not what they do," uttered as He hung on the Cross so long ago echo throughout the ages.

And to the Holy Spirit, who lives and breathes in us.

I dedicate all our efforts and prayers as we read God's Word prayerfully and are transformed by grace.

Acknowledgement

Thank you to my wife, Karen, for her support, patience and understanding. Many sacrifices are necessary for any endeavor of love. Our life has been such an endeavor, without her, this book would have never been possible. It is because of her companionship that I have been able to spend a life in ministry with teens in the Church.

Thank you to my children for all their understanding as my love has been shared with so many other teens in this world. Thank you for sharing me with them.

Thank you to the many adults and teens with whom I have ministered for four decades. You have been the inspiration for this work with the hope that we can sustain other teens on their journey and help them to love God with their whole heart, mind, soul, and strength, and their neighbor as themselves.

Thank you to my friends and family that have prayed for me, my family and my ministry.

Thank you, God, for giving us your only Son, out of love for us all and who is living in us still. Thank You for never breaking your promise to be with your Church throughout all time. Thank You for being our strength when we are weak and for guiding us to all truth and grace.

Introduction

I gave my life to Christ in the Summer of 1972 at Young Life camp in Saranac Village, NY. Words cannot describe what God's Spirit did for me that day and every day since.

Leading up to that day was a childhood full of many of the events that make up many teens' lives but my journey was also marked by severe losses and struggles. When I was about eight years old my father had a stroke which left him unable to work the rest of his life. We grew very close over the next four years which only made his sudden and unexpected death on August 14, 1967, so difficult.

I was affected so deeply. Normally a very emotional child, I could not cry at my father's funeral or for many years afterward. My prayer was first affected by my anger toward God over my inability to feel and express the pain I was experiencing. Later, I began to end each day by asking God if I could share my day with my dad. After sharing my day and saying good night, I would thank God for allowing me to talk to Dad.

Beginning my junior year in high school I started going to Tuesday night meetings with Young Life. I later went to camp and that is when my life changed. On Wednesday night was the Cross talk when we reflected on the tremendous act of love that Jesus suffered for us. The following night we each had the opportunity to give our lives to Christ. It was then that I stood and spoke the words allowed. They prayed for us and as they did the Spirit of God touched me in a way that I have never been touched before. Tears flowed and I experienced a healing that is so hard to describe.

I came home from camp and began reading the Bible from cover to cover and then again. Over the years, I found every answer, every support and direction for every challenge in my life. I looked back and could see how God was always active in my life helping me even when I didn't realize it. Because Scripture came to me so much I always had a desire to help others realize what a treasure Scripture is and how much help God gives us through it.

Among all the devotions in this book I hope you find assurance in the opening reflection for which the devotion is named. You are a gift from God. This is from a quiet time with Scripture I had while still in school. As you read from day to day, I hope Scripture comes to mean for you all that it has meant for me. I also hope you find in the Church the guidance you need to live a life filled with love and dedicated to building God's Kingdom right here where we live. God bless you as we journey together in Gods' Word.

Love in Jesus,

Pat Rinker

Preface

For many teens, the Scriptures are confusing, ancient, or just plain unrelated to problems such as divorce, rejection from friends, sexual temptations, or lack of self-identity. Though you may believe in God and enjoy some positive experiences of Church, your personal prayer life needs to grow along with your personal relationship with God. Reading the Bible can be more of a task than a pleasure and you may need help in applying the Scripture to what happens in your everyday life. *You're Worth It!* seeks to help you find in Scripture the guidance you need to build a strong relationship with God, to strengthen your self-worth, to help you deal with interrelational problems both in and outside your home, and give you an awareness of what your call to follow Christ looks like today. I believe daily prayer and Scripture are vital to your personal development. My hope is that *You're Worth It!* will help you discover the wealth of a strong relationship with God and his presence within you.

Daily prayer is not an easy discipline to develop. Having it be a constructive experience seems impossible, but it's not. These four steps will help you get started:

1. **Set up a daily appointment with God.** Give yourself at least fifteen minutes the same time each day and be there. The time you choose should be one that you will find easy to keep. Two good possible times are either when you first get up in the morning or before you go to sleep at night. If you have a better time, fine; just keep it. Having a consistent, special time will help you focus on prayer.

2. **The place you choose should be isolated and conducive to prayer.** Your thoughts can easily be distracted with much on your mind. As with time, having a consistent location will help you set the mood. The place itself will serve to remind you of why you are there.

3. **Center your thoughts on God.** Begin your prayer time by relaxing for a moment and clearing your mind of other thoughts. Ask God to speak to you during this time together.

Thank God for being present. There are many techniques that people use to pray. Some use music or periods of meditation. I suggest that you do whatever helps you to be in God's presence.

4. **Read the reflection.** It begins with *My Life*, to help you relate to the upcoming message. *Setting the Scene* helps you to understand where you are in the Scripture story, kind of like finding out where you are when you come in the middle of a movie.

Each daily devotion ends with a suggestion for prayer relative to the thought for the day and a *Journal/Activity*. The *Journal/Activity* offers you an opportunity to write or do something to experience more deeply the reflection of the day.

After finishing the daily devotion, you may want to continue with prayer. If you have any needs, bring them to God. One tool I use is a prayer list, containing those people and things for which others have asked me to pray. When finished, remember to thank God for the time you had together. Commit your day to God.

I recommend that *You're Worth It!* be read in the order that it's written. Each day is built on the previous day. Individual areas of need are addressed in blocks of several daily readings.

If you do require special help in an area of your life, consult the outline of the devotional. Each day's theme is indicated. The entire devotional is also outlined in order for you to zero in on a particular area of need.

I pray that this devotional, in combination with support within your church, will enable you to recognize what a valuable person you are. You are created in God's image and are worth everything he has done for you. You are called to be the person that God created you to be. It is a calling that can be fulfilled as you learn to dwell in God's love and allow the Holy Spirit to dwell in you. Draw on the strength of God as you cope with problems. Celebrate with God the good things that have happened and learn to recognize the extent of God's love for you. In reflecting daily on the thoughts of this devotional, I pray that you'll be able to look at who you are, and God's love for you, and say, "I'm worth it!"

Love in Jesus,

Pat Rinker

Table of Contents

I. Am I Worth It? (Basis of your concept of self-worth and
foundation of your relationship with God.) 17

Matthew 13:44-46 .... The Pearl of Great Price 18
Jeremiah 1:4-8 .... Who Me? 20
1 Timothy 4:12-16 .... Hang in There! 22
Numbers 13:25-33 .... Accentuate the Positive 24
1 Corinthians 12:4-7 .... You're Indispensable 26
Philippians 4:13 .... I Can Do It! 28
Romans 7:14-25 .... Keep on Trying 30
Matthew 26:69–75 .... So Who's Perfect? 32
2 Corinthians 5:15-21 .. We're a New Creation 34
Galatians 2:15-21 .... Internal Presence 36
Psalm 139:1-6 .... Getting to Know You 38
Romans 8:35-39 .... God Will Always Be There 40
1 Corinthians 10:13 ...... No Situation Too Tough 42
1 John 4:17-18 .... Confidence Based on Love 44
Genesis 1:26-27 .... You Are Made in God's Image 46

II. Alignation from God (A look at our separation from
God and keys to be reunited with Him.) 48

2 Kings 17:13-15 .... Bridging the Gap 50
Luke 15:1-7 .... God's Attitude toward You 52
2 Samuel 11:4-6, 12-17 ... Facing Up to My Mistake 54
Psalm 32:3-7 .... I'm Glad I Got That Off My Chest 56
Matthew 4:1-11 .... Dealing with Temptation 58
Matthew 6:13 .... The Wrong Place at the Wrong Time 60
Romans 8:5-8 .... You Will Be What You Are Becoming 62
Luke 9:57-62 .... No Strings Attached 64
Micah 6:8 .... What Does God Ask of Me? 66
Matthew 6:33-34 .... The Lighthouse in the Storm 68
Luke 24:30-35 .... God Reveals Himself to You 70
Matthew 6:9-13 .... But How Do I Pray? 72
1 Kings 19:9-13 .... Learning to Listen to God 74
2 Timothy 3:16-17 .... The Purpose of God's Word 76

III. Alienation within Family (A look at the different conflicts which arise within family – sibling conflict, communication breakdown, divorce, moving – and finding consolation and guidance in God's Word.) 79

Genesis 1:1-5 .... God Brings Order from Chaos 80
Joshua 5:13-15 .... Don't Take Sides 82
Joshua 6:15-20 .... Rebuilding Relationships 84
Matthew 11:28-30 .... Don't Carry the Load 86
Genesis 45:1-15 .... Family Reunion 88
Matthew 14:25-30 .... How Do I Hang in There? 90
John 11:17-25, 39-44 .. Reach Out 92
Philippians 1:20-26 ...... My Purpose for Life 94
Genesis 12:1-5 .... Moving On Again 96
Genesis 28:13-15 .... God Is There Beside Me 98
Luke 15:25-32 .... My Parents Don't Understand Me! 100
Acts 7:54-60 .... Healing after Rejection 102
Romans 8:14-17 .... God's Child by Adoption 104
Matthew 7:1-5 .... My Parents Are, Too 106
Luke 2:48-52 .... I'm Getting Older, Mom and Dad! 108
Mark 4:30-34 .... Making New Beginnings 110
Luke 10:38-42 .... Learning to Listen 112
1 Corinthians 13:4-7 .... Love Is the Key 114
Proverbs 10:14 .... The Power of the Tongue 116
Hebrews 12:5-6 .... A Parent Who Cares 118
Matthew 7:12 .... A Good Philosophy toward Parents 120
Jonah 1:1-3, 10-12 .... Authority 122
Jonah 3:6-10 .... Maybe They Had a Point 124
Jonah 4:5-11 .... Learning the Easy Way 126
Psalm 100 .... What Should I Be Thankful For? 128

IV. Alienation from Friends (A look at the walls we build between friends and the manner in which we let potential friendships dictate behavior. Keys for friendships are developed.) 131

Matthew 26:31-35 .... Building Friendship 132
Luke 22:47-53 .... Betrayed Me with a Kiss 134
Psalm 12 .... Good Outweighs the Bad 136
Matthew 18:15-18 .... Keep It between the Two of You 138
Genesis 37:3-4 .... Be Thankful for What You Have 140

Matthew 1:18-25..........Get the Facts First..142
Genesis 37:5-8 ....Don't Drown Them with Your Feelings........ 144
Galatians 6:1-2 ....Help Each Other Along..............................146
John 15:9-12 ....The Degree of Our Love............................148
Matthew 18:21-35 ....Learning to Forgive Is Important 150
1 Corinthians 13:11-13...Adjusting to Changing Friends.............152
1 Samuel 17:38-40.......Be Honest About Who You Are..............154
1 Samuel 20:38-42.......Saying Good-Bye.....................................156
Matthew 28:20 ....God Is with You 158

V. Dating Relationships (Getting into the perspective of friendships that grow.)..161

2 Corinthians 6:14–18...Have Something in Common 162
1 John 2:15-17 ....How Much Has Really Changed? 164
Genesis 2:18....................Sex Was God's Idea..............................166
Genesis 2:21-24 ....Enjoy It within Commitment...................168
Matthew 5:27-30..........Keep It Natural......................................170
Romans 6:12....................It's Worth Waiting For 172
John 8:3-11 ....What If I Didn't Wait?............................174
Judges 16:4-5................The Right Way to Break Up...................176
Genesis 19:20-26 ....A New Day...178

VI. Fellowship in God's Family (The value of Church community and the stability it offers with others and with God.)..................181

Matthew 12:46-50 ....I Know You..182
John 15:1-15..................How Does It Help Me?...........................184
Luke 19:1-10..................The Good in Each of Us.........................186
Acts 4:32-35..................They Know How I Feel 188
Revelation 21:1-7 ....Thanks God, I Needed That!.................190

VII. Christian Discipleship (Here we will examine God's call to be His witnesses to others.)............193

James 2:14-17.............Don't Just Say It..........................194
Matthew 5:3-12 ....The Blessings Will Come.............196
Matthew 9:35-38.........You're Really Needed 198
Ezekiel 3:17-21 ....My Brother's Keeper...................200
John 13:3-15.................Learning to Serve.......................202
Exodus 18:13-22 ....You Can Make a Difference 204
Numbers 30:2-3 ....Make a Commitment that Lasts.....206

VIII. Counting the Cost (Examining both the proper steps necessary to be Christ's disciples and the costs that lie ahead, we get a realistic view of God's call.)............209

Deuteronomy 9:1-6......Depend on God!.......................... 210
Matthew 16:1-4 ....Trust...212
Acts 16:16-19................Sensitivity 214
Matthew 10:16-20........God Will Give Us Words to Speak....216
Matthew 21:12-13 ....A Little Anger Can Be Good..........218
Judges 7:2-7 ....Quality, Not Quantity...................220
Genesis 15:1-6.............There Will Be Doubts...................222
Acts 2:1-8.......................The Source Can Come Through.....224

IX. Social Issues (Eventually discipleship must be applied to the society in which we live, if we are to truly love our neighbor. We will examine those issues which must be confronted in the name of Christ, if we are to fulfill His command.)............227

Luke 6:27-29 ....Turning the Cheek........................228
Psalm 41:1-4.................Reaching Out to the Poor............230
Isaiah 31:1-3.................Even Israel Needed Correction 232
Mark 12:29-31 ....The Call of Love 234
Acts 10:34-35................Color-Blind Faith..........................236
Romans 14:4-7 ....Christian Unity.............................238
Luke 4:16-19 ....The Call of Christian Witness 240
Matthew 15:1-6...........Love Begins at Home....................242

X. Getting Back to God (The key to solutions, of all the problems we face, lies in getting back to God. Here we summarize the key ingredients of our relationship with God.) 245

Revelation 3:15-20 .... Don't Straddle the Fence 246
Romans 10:6-13 .... He's as Near as My Heart 248
John 3:16-21 .... Believe in Him Who Loves You 250
Exodus 3:1-5 .... How Is God Trying to Get Your Attention? ...252
Philippians 2:6-11 .... Humbling Ourselves in Order to Rise 254
John 17:20-23 .... Jesus' Prayer for Us 256
Matthew 16:13-17 .... Who Do I Say He Is? 258
Hebrews 11:1-3 .... What Does It Mean to Believe? 260
Galatians 5:22-26 .... Evidence of Jesus in Me 262
Exodus 33:12-17 .... God, My Closest Friend 264
Ephesians 6:10-17 .... Standing Strong in Christ 266
Matthew 18:19-20 .... Standing Together, You and I 268
Luke 8:1-15 .... How Will I Make It? 270
Romans 8:28-31 .... We Will Make It! 272
Matthew 13:44-46 .... You're Worth It! 274

Chapter 1
Am I Worth It?

In Christ who is the source of my strength,
I have strength for everything. (Phil 4:13)

The Pearl of Great Price

My Life

Can you think of a place or experience so great that you have never forgotten it? It's a memory you treasure so much you would give up almost anything to have it again.

Setting the Scene

Jesus told many parables to the people of his day to help them understand the good news he came to share. In this parable we commonly understand the treasure to symbolize the Kingdom of God. But what if you were the treasure that Jesus wanted so much?

Matthew 13:44-46

Reflection

Can you sense the excitement these men must have felt for their discovered treasure? The sense of satisfaction in finding it is a feeling they will long remember. There will always be something inside of them that wants that experience again and if they could really have it, they would sacrifice for it.

Jesus obviously felt that same way for us. He did exactly what these men did. He gave up everything he had, his place in heaven and all the honor it held, and became like you and me. He rejected all material gain, and throughout the course of his ministry never had a home. He eventually was denied by his most loyal follower, betrayed by another, and died. All this Jesus willingly did so he could have his buried treasure, his Pearl of Great Price.

You are that pearl. God looked down on you, with all the problems you incur during your life, and was driven by his love for you to sacrifice all he had. He counted the cost and decided you were worth it. You were worth the life of the Son of God. That's your value. You're not cheap. You're priceless! You are the Pearl of Great Price and that's God's opinion. Now who knows better than God?

Take It to God

Pray today that God may help you to see your value and your

goodness. Ask God to develop in you a measure of love for yourself as he himself loves you.

Journal/Activity

Make a list of ten good qualities you see in yourself. If you have trouble thinking of ten qualities, call a friend or talk to a parent or other family member. You are a buried treasure. Thank God for each quality you record.

_____

_____

_____

_____

_____

_____

_____

_____

_____

_____

_____

_____

_____

_____

_____

_____

_____

_____

Who Me?

My Life

Have you ever been called upon in class and you wished the teacher had asked someone else? Have you ever been in a situation where everyone was older than you and you felt the need to say something but because you were so young you didn't speak up?

Setting the Scene

That is where we find Jeremiah in this passage. He is a very young man and God is calling him to be his messenger to the Israelites. They often stray from living God's way and someone needs to remind them to be faithful to God. So God calls Jeremiah and he responds.

Jeremiah 1:4-8

Reflection

"I know not how to speak; I am too young." Seems like a pretty good excuse, but God doesn't buy it. He knows Jeremiah too well. He made him and knows his potential, so He sends Jeremiah on to be a prophet despite his age or lack of confidence.

God knows you and your potential, too. So many times we give up on ourselves and we don't push for our full potential. We don't try to do well in school, so not trying will be our excuse for failure. We don't go out for a sport we like, so being cut won't be our embarrassing moment. We refrain from speaking when something's wrong, because no one will listen anyway.

Take It to God

What is God calling you to do? What interests do you have that you can pursue? God was with Jeremiah, and God is with you too. Pray today that God will give you confidence in yourself and teach you not to use excuses, but to keep on trying.

Journal/Activity

Look back at the qualities from the journal activity from the first reflection in this section. Go through each quality and write down how these qualities can help you to achieve a goal or pursue an interest.

_____

_____

_____

_____

_____

_____

_____

_____

_____

_____

_____

_____

_____

_____

_____

_____

_____

_____

_____

_____

_____

Hang In There!

My Life

Have you ever been frustrated because adults – parents, teachers, or anyone else – would not listen to your side of the story?

Setting the Scene

You know how Timothy must have felt. You also have to give Paul a big cheer for standing by Timothy with encouraging words. Timothy was a young man who was called to take on a leadership role in a small first-century Church because there was no one else to lead.

1 Timothy 4:12-16

Reflection

There are times when, because of your youth, people just aren't going to listen. At this point talk is cheap. You have to back it up with action. Paul encouraged Timothy to do just that. Be an example for others and hang in there. Keep praying and by your progress you will convince others.

How can you apply this lesson in your life? Have you tried to convince your parents that they can trust you? Be trustworthy. Have you tried to convince the coach you should be on the team? Practice that much harder and show him next year. How about getting a "B" in algebra instead of a "C"?

Having integrity and trusting in your own ability don't come easily. You're not the first to realize that. Timothy did and he hung tough and made it. You are gifted according to your position in life, as he was. Take Paul's advice and don't be discouraged, "but set an example for those who believe, in speech, conduct, love, faith, and purity."

Take It to God

Pray that God might help you to be strong, especially when people put you down because of your age. Pray for patience that the good of tomorrow will get you through the struggle of today.

You're Worth It!

Journal/Activity

Record an experience in which you felt discouraged. Now imagine that someone is coming to you and sharing this same experience with you. What words of encouragement would you give that person? What words of encouragement would Paul speak to you today?

_____

_____

_____

_____

_____

_____

_____

_____

_____

_____

_____

_____

_____

_____

_____

_____

_____

_____

_____

_____

Accentuate the Positive

My Life

Do you ever find yourself so pessimistic that you believe the worst?

Setting the Scene

That's where we find ourselves in this passage. After being freed from slavery in Egypt, parting the Red Sea, going through the desert, and receiving the commandments from God, the Israelites would not enter the Promised Land which they knew was everything they had hoped for. If God had done all these great works, what was keeping them from entering?

Numbers 13:25-33

Reflection

The Israelites put more faith in the negative report than in the positive. You and I probably do this too. They saw a land of milk and honey but chose to ignore it. Let's not ignore the positives in our life. Have confidence that you can pass that hard class or that the person you've been wanting to ask out just might say yes. There are so many goals that are set before you in your life. Do you believe people who constantly say you can't or listen to those who encourage you to go on?

The Israelites didn't listen to the good report and they ended up in the desert for 40 years before finally entering the land. What are you going to put off until it's too late? What are you going to believe about yourself? Start ignoring some of the put-downs you might hear today and put stock in words that encourage you.

Take It to God

Pray that God will increase your confidence and learn to listen to positive things and gain a positive outlook on yourself and on life.

Journal/Activity

If you have a few good friends you can trust, ask them to write down the ways in which you are positive.

You're Indispensable

My Life

Have you ever been involved with anything where you were the one who worked behind the scenes while someone else got all the credit?

Setting the Scene

Here we read part of Paul's first letter to a group of Christians who live in Corinth. They are young Christians whom Paul has to remind to live the Christian life and to use their gifts for the benefit of each other.

1 Corinthians 12:4-7

Reflection

When I was a senior in high school, I played on our varsity basketball team. I was a third-string guard. That means I played in practice, but not in games. A lot of people in my position probably would have quit, but God helped me maintain a positive attitude, so I always worked hard in practice.

The third string always played the defense of the next team on the schedule in practice so the first string could learn how to score against it. About halfway through the season our starting guard came up to me after practice and told me that it was more difficult to score on me in practice than it was in the game. He told me how well I played defense and that he respected the effort I put out.

That meant a lot to me. Sure I would have rather played in games and I felt I was able to, but since I couldn't, I wanted to know that I made a difference. I counted. As one part of the whole team I made it better by being there with a positive attitude.

No matter what your role is in your church youth group, at school, at home, or anywhere, you are indispensable! God has gifted you and has you there for a purpose.

Take It to God

Pray that God will enable you to see your value to classmates, family members, and others. Seek His help in maintaining a positive attitude, even if your part seems small.

Journal/Activity

Think of someone you know who exhibits a positive attitude toward their work or something else that they do. Ask them what motivates them to do what they do. Consider how their attitude affects how they feel about their work.

_____

_____

_____

_____

_____

_____

_____

_____

_____

_____

_____

_____

_____

_____

_____

_____

_____

_____

_____

_____

I Can Do It!

My Life

Have you ever felt so whipped that you just couldn't continue?

Setting the Scene

In this letter to the Christians in Philippi, Paul has already shared with them his struggle in prison and how his faith and commitment to leading others to Christ gives him reason to continue his mission.

Philippians 4:13

Reflection

If you've accepted what has been said in the previous reflections to this point, it shouldn't really be hard to believe that you can accomplish many things. For starters, your initial price tag was the life of the Son of God. That makes you pretty good already. Second, God has given you gifts, many of them according to where you are and where you are going. It's up to you to develop them and use them for good.

That brings us to the point of success. No, God isn't saying you can run the 100-yard dash in ten seconds. He is saying that you have abilities which were given to you so that you can play an important role in the life of your family, your school, and anywhere else you find yourself. God is also saying that he is your source of strength and with the two of you working together, you will succeed.

The question is: In what will you succeed? The first thing you are called to succeed in is being you. Be who God created you to be.

Take It to God

Pray that God will be with you in all you do and that you may be with him, for God is your strength and Lord. Pray also that you will be thankful for who you are and for the important things you know you can do.

Journal/Activity

Write down one thing that you have been putting off. Record what it will take to accomplish this task. Write down what qualities or gifts you have now that will help you to accomplish the goal. Think about what skills or knowledge you still need. Write down how you will obtain the knowledge and skill and who can help you. Take the steps you have written and share them with a parent, teacher, or someone else you trust. Listen for other ideas and be prepared to begin accomplishing your goal.

Keep On Trying

My Life

Are there certain areas of your life with which you constantly struggle? Do you want to do better but you falter again and again?

Setting the Scene

Earlier in this letter to the Romans, Paul writes about how God has reached out to us and given us the faith we need. But in this passage it is clear that we soon slip into the same wretched sinner image that Paul so effectively describes.

Romans 7:14-25

Reflection

Are we so bad if the desire to do good is there? No! We just have a common condition of all humankind. We have a disease called sin. So what do we do about it? What is this thing, sin, anyway?

The Greek word in the New Testament most often used for sin is *armatia*. This word is also used in archery to describe a shot that is off the mark. Sin, then, can be said to refer to you and me not quite being on target in our relationship with God and others. The point is that if you want to be a good archer you don't just pick up a bow and start shooting bullseyes. You keep practicing and you get better. We need to keep our focus on that desire to do good and recognize that it takes time to become the person God created us to be.

Take It to God

Pray that God may give you the patience not to give up on yourself and the desire to continue to strive to do the right thing.

Journal/Activity

Think of an area in your life in which you struggle. Rather than focus on the struggle, picture yourself as you would imagine you would be after you have overcome that struggle. That's the bullseye. Dream a little. Think about how this would affect your relationships with others. How would this affect your life? Dreams help us to accomplish great things. Treasure your dreams.

_____

_____

_____

_____

_____

_____

_____

_____

_____

_____

_____

_____

_____

_____

_____

_____

_____

_____

_____

_____

_____

So Who's Perfect?

My Life

Have you been afraid of what people will think? Have you ever denied being religious, being a Christian, or knowing Jesus?

Setting the Scene

In this passage, Jesus has just been arrested and Peter is outside the place where Jesus is being questioned. Peter has just spent three years with Jesus, believing Jesus to be the Messiah and witnessing all that Jesus said and did.

Matthew 26:69-75

Reflection

It is amazing when you think about it. At the time when Jesus needed support most, Peter left him. One of the neat things about the Bible is that it doesn't hide the sins of its human heroes. We all know after reading the book that no one is perfect. We all, at one time or another, miss the mark. We fail to realize our potential and act, instead, out of fear or disbelief. Peter repented and kept trying.

Take It to God

We're all in the same boat, so we all need to pray for many of the same things. Pray that God may allow you to realize that your mistakes don't diminish your value. You're an unpolished gem who needs to be refined. Peter's calling was that of the first pope. If he could fulfill his calling after deserting Christ, surely you can too!

Journal/Activity

Write down a mistake you made once. What have you learned from the mistake? Write down the situation and how you would handle it differently now. Having learned from your mistake, write yourself a note of forgiveness. Leave the mistake behind but remember what you learned.

We're a New Creation

My Life

"She's only human" or "That's Charlie, he'll never change" are statements that you may have heard before. Do they hold you back and make you believe you can't grow?

Setting the Scene

Again Paul writes to the Corinthian community, a community often in conflict and straying from the messages they have heard. Here Paul appeals to them to continue the process of true spiritual growth.

2 Corinthians 5:15-21

Reflection

We're a new creation! What does that mean?

It means that God is at work! He's giving us a new beginning. We no longer have to rely on ourselves alone. Charlie can change. He can grow and so can you. Little by little, old habits can diminish and new ones form, habits that are on target with the person you were created to be. Not only does God forgive us, but the same power that raised Jesus from the dead is also at work helping you to become new.

What old habits do you wish to change, but thought you never could? You may not like your constant swearing, but it's hard to break because of your temper. Ask God to help you control your emotions so that what you say can be constructive and to the point. You may be tempted to cheat on tests at school. Ask God to help you to be honest with others about what you can do and to have the discipline to do it.

Take It to God

There are so many tough areas that you have to deal with and your peers may make it harder. Realize that you finally have the means to change and grow and be all that you can be. Pray that God may constantly stir your heart toward him and his way.

Journal/Activity

Take time to take a walk outside. Look at the nature that is around you. Even if you live in a city, there are areas of grass or trees or some form of life. Consider how nature changes throughout the seasons. Focus on one thing and consider how it changes during Fall and Winter and how something new happens in the Spring. All things change and become new, including you and me.

_____

_____

_____

_____

_____

_____

_____

_____

_____

_____

_____

_____

_____

_____

_____

_____

_____

Internal Presence

My Life

Have you ever felt an inner peace that gave you the confidence to do what is right even when those around you didn't?

Setting the Scene

In this letter from Paul to the Galatians he talks to them about their failure to be faithful to the call to follow Christ. He shares with them that inner peace that comes from Christ.

Galatians 2:15-21

Reflection

Internal Presence

> The Power of the changing tide,
> the rush of the open sea,
> the vastness of the night lit sky,
> as far as the eye can see,
> the depth of the clear blue ocean,
> the coolness of the mountain stream,
> the gentle touch of God's mighty hand,
> painting pictures of which we dream.
> By His Word has this been given,
> spoken and it came to be,
> from chaos came order and darkness light
> and life for eternity.
> But of all of His works I treasure
> the beauty of the Master's art
> is the Presence of His living in me
> His dwelling in my heart.

Take It to God

Pray that the life-giving presence of Jesus Christ may live in you. God can live in you and the powerful love that created life and all that is will reside in you. He will enable you to live for Him.

You're Worth It!

Journal/Activity

Take some time the next evening that there is a clear sky and go outside and look at the stars. Do this for at least five minutes. Imagine the God who made all of that and know that God is as close as your heart.

Getting to Know You

My Life

Do you have a close friend who knows you better than anybody and is there for you no matter what happens?

Setting the Scene

The Psalms reflect on times when we felt alone and everyone was against us. They celebrate the joy of knowing that God helps us in our great need. In this psalm the psalmist reflects upon the presence of God in our lives.

Psalm 139:1-6

Reflection

My first reaction is mixed as I consider the ramifications of God knowing me so well. There are a few unclean thoughts in there, a few things that maybe I would not want others to know. You might have that reaction, too. Can the God who knows me so well still love me?

Apparently, yes. For there is nowhere we can go to escape God's presence. He knows us before we were made and knows us better than we know ourselves. He still died for us, too. That says a lot.

First, it shows how much God loves each of us. He doesn't judge you for things you have done that weren't quite right, but sees you in your struggle and still helps. He seeks to guide you and probe you and show you where you are right.

Second, it shows that God sees more good there than you or I do. You sell yourself short when you put yourself down. You don't realize the goodness that is there. God does. He knows absolutely everything there is to know about you and still continues to love you.

As you continue to mature, you will understand yourself more fully. You will see your mistakes but you will see your potential as well. That potential is only a glimpse of what God sees.

Take It to God

Pray that God will probe you to show you where you should go next. Ask God to guide you in the right direction and be open to

You're Worth It!

embrace what God reveals to you.

Journal/Activity

Ask a parent to share with you the experience of seeing you take your first steps. Listen for the feelings they felt. Were they happy about your steps or upset that you fell? If you wish, record what they said about your first steps and remember we are all learning to walk with God every day.

_____

_____

_____

_____

_____

_____

_____

_____

_____

_____

_____

_____

_____

_____

_____

_____

_____

_____

_____

God Will Always Be There

My Life

Do you ever worry that your relationship with God won't last? You may fear at times that maybe the circumstances of life may be stronger than the bond you have with God.

Setting the Scene

In this passage from Romans it clearly states the depth of God's love and that nothing is stronger. It comes after Paul reflects upon his frustrations in failing God and in feeling a sense that all is lost.

Romans 8:35-39

What distress have you had in life that tested your hope for life? From whom do you fear rejection the most, and why do you fear their rejection? What needs do you have that you fear will not be met? Who can bring you harm so great that God will not be there?

This passage addresses Christians who may have felt a loss of hope and security. It encourages them, and you, to:

- Let your essence of life be God and your hope will not be diminished.
- Let your closest friend be Jesus, who died for you for he will never reject you.
- Let your needs and security rest in what God offers you for God will never withdraw his hand.
- Let God's love be ever on your mind for all that he gives you is sustained by it and nothing is stronger.

Take It to God

Pray that your awareness of God's love for you grows for it is your strength and it will sustain in you the knowledge that there isn't anything that you will experience today that God's love cannot conquer.

Journal/Activity

At the cross Jesus said, in reference to those who crucified him,

"Father, forgive them, they know not what they do." Not even that could separate them from God's love for them. If you do not have a cross, draw one in your journal or pick one up in a store or at your church. Keep it as a reminder that God will always love you.

_____

_____

_____

_____

_____

_____

_____

_____

_____

_____

_____

_____

_____

_____

_____

_____

_____

_____

No Situation Too Tough

My Life

Have you ever asked God the question, "Why me?" Many people have. It seems to be making the assumption that someone else isn't experiencing problems and God is picking on you.

Setting the Scene

Back to Paul's first letter to the Corinthians. After giving much direction to the community, he now gives them encouragement that God will see them through the tough times.

1 Corinthians 10:13

Reflection

Not only does God allow you to experience life's difficulties, but God knows your limitations and gives you the means to make it through the problem and know the time to leave it. The questions now come back to you.

Do you place yourself in tempting situations and then experience disappointment for not being strong enough? Are there habits from your past that continue to place you in trying situations with others?

Nothing will come to you that, with God's strength, you can't handle or avoid. Have you tempted fate yourself and then when it comes time to reap what you sow, you cry out, "Why me?"

Take It to God

In trying situations depend on God and seek God's guidance. Pray that God will show you any sins that you may be guilty of what may have caused you problems. Trust that God will deliver. Also know that God does not punish you vengefully with disasters. The trials I speak of here are those within the context of relationships with others. Pray for God's peace, for God will be there!

Journal/Activity

If you can, watch the movie "Rudy." It is an inspirational true story of a young man who overcame many obstacles to accomplish his dreams. Let the story inspire you to believe in your abilities and in God in overcoming the trials of your life.

Confidence Based on Love

My Life

Think of a time when you were little and you were afraid. How many times did you call out to Mom or Dad or someone else you trusted when you were afraid? When they came close and were there for you were you less afraid? Somehow their loving presence helped you to feel secure. Love casts out all fear.

Setting the Scene

In this letter, attributed to the apostle John, John calls on an early Christian community to believe in the core of Christian doctrine which at its base is founded on a deep love and faith in Jesus Christ.

1 John 4: 17-18

Reflection

I have a strong fear of heights. My first house was a two-story house and it needed painting. I confided to a close friend my fear. We set up two extension ladders. He went up one and I went up the other. His presence helped me to overcome my fear. The next time I painted that house by myself.

Experiencing the loving presence of Christ can have the same effect on our lives. The more we experience him and know his love, the more confidence we have in living the Christian life.

Take It to God

We don't always realize it, but God is always with us. The stronger our faith in God's presence, the less we fear. Pray that God will draw you closer to him. As you are drawn closer, pray that your capacity to love will grow and your level of fear will diminish.

Journal/Activity

Plan on going to a store or another public place where you can observe small children with their parents. Watch for occasions when the children call out to their parents when they feel insecure. See in their parents' response examples of how their presence brings security to the child. Know that God is always present in your life.

You Are Made in God's Image

My Life

Have you ever played with a little windup doll? You pulled the string and it would say, "I love you." Did you feel loved?

Setting the Scene

In this early account of the creation story the author emphasizes that we are the intended creation of a loving God. God purposely created us in the male/female image of God.

Genesis 1:26-27

Reflection

God could have created you like the doll. Everything that God wanted the doll to do he would program it to function in just that way. It could water the plants, take care of the animals, not pollute the atmosphere, and it certainly would love all the other dolls, and the other dolls would love it back. This is all very true if you accept the fact that love can be programmed.

To be made in God's image demanded the ability to love of our own accord. That also means we would have the choice not to love, for if there isn't that opportunity then there isn't the choice to love either. This may sound risky, but it would only be considered a risk if you don't take into account that we were made in God's image.

So we do go through a struggle in becoming a better reflection of God's love. Down through the years we have failed. God saw that the spirit of life he breathed into us has faded, so he gave us new life in Christ. The purpose was to allow us to grow back into the image, perfectly reflecting God. To be that image, we will need to grow to the point where we do all things that the doll could do but we do it by our own choice. The most important duty of all is to look to our creator and say, "I love you."

Take It to God

Pray that God's Spirit may revive in you that image of God and that you may grow more capable of loving God and others.

Journal/Activity

Pretend you are God and write down how you would create someone in your image. Think of all the good qualities you would give this creation. Write down how you would take care of this creature. What would you provide? What would you be willing to do for this creature? Now write down the qualities that God has created in you, how God has provided for you and what God has done for you.

_____

_____

_____

_____

_____

_____

_____

_____

_____

_____

_____

_____

_____

_____

_____

_____

_____

_____

_____

You're Worth It!

Chapter II
Alienation from God

*Seek first the kingdom of God and his righteousness,
and all these things will be given you besides.* (Mt 6:33)

Bridging the Gap

My Life

Did you ever meet someone you were attracted to but thought they would never be interested in you? Then you never told them how you felt or showed interest because of your fear of rejection?

Setting the Scene

In the history of the Israelites there was always the tension between remaining faithful to their God or turning away from God and worshiping the God of their enemy. God often sent prophets to warn the people to return to their God.

2 Kings 17:13-15

Reflection

Our separation from God is most distant when that separation is caused by the way we live our lives. Sin is the rushing torrent that flows between God and us. The more sin we pump into that river, the deeper and wider it gets. More and more we fear crossing as we continue to wait. It never seems to narrow. It never seems safe. We stop on our distant shore, not happy with the life we have, yet still planting seeds of division keeping us from God.

The Israelites got caught up in that torrent, generation after generation. As a people they rejected God so continuously that finally their sin led to the exile of their people. God drew them from exile in Egypt and gave them the Promised Land, but their constant compromise of loyalty to God led to another exile. Only the tribe of Judah remained. Even the Israelite people were divided one from another.

Take It to God

Pray that God will instill in you a desire to break that habit of sin in your life. Begin with one area of your life and seek God's help in leading a better life. Slowly you will begin to experience a closer relationship with God as your ways become more in line with the life of Christ.

Journal/Activity

Often the habit of sin is nurtured by the situations in which we place ourselves. Make a list of the people, places, and things that are around when you fall into the habit of sin you prayed about. Next to each item on the list record how you will avoid that situation or place and change your relationship with that person in order to avoid the sin that separates you from the one who loves you most, God.

_____

_____

_____

_____

_____

_____

_____

_____

_____

_____

_____

_____

_____

_____

_____

_____

_____

_____

_____

God's Attitude toward You

My Life

Have you ever been at a party or another gathering of people you know and there at the same place was a former close friend? You haven't spoken in quite some time. A misunderstanding led to some bitter feelings and you couldn't handle talking to each other because the feelings would always emerge.

Setting the Scene

In this chapter of Luke Jesus shares a series of parables that illustrate how our loving God reaches out to those who are separated from him.

Luke 15:1-7

Reflection

Think back to the former close friend you saw at the party. Would you leave behind all your friends at this party and go off to reconcile with your old friend?

That is what Jesus does in this parable. Just as you would have great joy in regaining an old friendship, so Jesus feels the same way for us when, because of sin, we haven't spoken to him for a while. He looks for opportunities to bring us back together. He will remind us of his presence through others, or just within ourselves. Jesus is our friend. He's one who will never cause division between you and others, but only seeks to bring you back together again.

Take It to God

In your prayer time today, reflect on the love that sent Jesus, the shepherd, after his lost sheep and dwell on the attitude he must have toward us when we are lost as well.

Journal/Activity

Think of a time when you have lost something of value and after your search, you find it. Think of the feelings you had. Write down the words that describe your feelings at that time. These may be some of the words that describe how Jesus feels for you when you return to him.

_____

_____

_____

_____

_____

_____

_____

_____

_____

_____

_____

_____

_____

_____

_____

_____

_____

_____

_____

_____

_____

_____

Facing Up to My Mistake

My Life

Have you ever done something that you're so ashamed of that you don't want anyone else to know?

Setting the Scene

We begin this scene with David having taken notice of a beautiful woman who is married to one of the soldiers in his army. This soldier was sent away to battle for his king. David has seen her bathing and is captivated by her beauty.

2 Samuel 11:4-6, 12-17

Reflection

David wouldn't feel out of place today. We've become quite proficient at hiding the things we do, convincing ourselves that it is okay. We rationalize enough until we deaden our conscience and sadly, this leads to deeper offenses.

David fell into that same trap. He started with adultery and ended up with murder. He could have faced up to his initial sin, but that's hard to do. He sought the easy solution and ended up with a more difficult dilemma.

When have you done something that you rationalized rather than face your guilt or worse yet, face God? We feel like the kid who got caught with his hand in the cookie jar, so we try and hide the cookie. It doesn't work. Denial leads to more sin.

What in our society do we rationalize about and don't admit our mistakes? Sin leads to sin, if we don't face up to what we have done. What sin are you covering up, not dealing with, and pretending that it's okay?

Take it to God

Pray that God will give you the courage to stop covering up your sins, so you are not led into greater problems. Recognize that God is there to heal you, not condemn you for what you have done. You do not need to be ashamed before God because God still loves you. God

You're Worth It!

has provided you a grace-filled way to confess and be healed in the Sacrament of Reconciliation. There is no better place to face up to your mistake and be forgiven.

Journal/Activity

Nature is a beautiful example of today's reflection. When we pollute the environment and try to cover it up, it only gets worse. So it is with us. Basically, you are incredibly beautiful, just like the rest of God's creation. Go for a walk this evening and consider the beauty of God's creation. Realize that as pollution affects creation so sin affects us. Thank God for the beautiful person you are.

I'm Glad I Got That Off My Chest

My Life

Have you ever felt anxious because you didn't know the truth? Once you know the truth, even if it's not the best news, you feel some relief. You need to know where you stand so you can deal with it, whatever it is.

Setting the Scene

The Psalms are a collection of liturgical hymns and public and personal prayers from many years of the Israelite tradition. This psalm is attributed to David and is believed to be a part of his response to God when he faced up to what he had done to Uriah.

Psalm 32:3-7

Reflection

When I was a senior in high school I had a crush on a classmate. I thought about her a lot and went over to her house to see her often. Over the course of time, I asked her out several times and with each invitation came a reason why she couldn't go out, with the assurance that she really did want to go out with me. I asked her straight out if she didn't want to go out with me, but she assured me that she did. As the relationship continued, the cold shoulder began and my anxiety increased. I finally called her and told her how I felt and said our friendship was over if she wouldn't be honest with me. Our friendship was of enough value to her that she finally told me that she did not want to date me. You would think I would have been crushed, but I was glad to finally clear the air.

With any relationship, you have to be honest. You must be honest with your feelings and share them with the other person. It's the same way with God. We have to be open and not hold anything back. When we confess our sins and receive God's forgiveness there is a tremendous release. We don't have to carry the burdens. We can seek our God and he will be there to support us.

Take It to God

I know that both my high school friend and I felt better after our conversation. I know I've felt better after being straight with God. Seek God whenever you fall. Give God your sorrow and frustration and pray for forgiveness. Your burden of anxiety will be lifted and God's peace will be with you. Talk to God now about anything in your life that you have avoided. Be straight with God.

Journal/Activity

Sometimes we owe someone an apology but we don't want to see them again. It is so important to speak your true feelings. If you have someone in your life who deserves an apology, sit down and write them a letter sharing your feelings.

Dealing with Temptation

My Life

When are you weak? When have you purposefully placed yourself in a trying situation with an attitude that you cannot fail? When are you tempted to seek popularity or acceptance from a certain group while failing to be true to your own convictions?

Setting the Scene

Here Jesus is about to begin his public ministry, but before he does he goes off to pray. During his prayer he is confronted with the same basic temptations that in some way confront you and me.

Matthew 4:1-11

Reflection

There are several characteristics of temptation here with which we can all identify. The question is, What are we learning from Jesus' response?

Temptation is often the strongest when we are at our weakest point. Satan approaches Jesus with food when he is hungry. Jesus responds that his nourishment comes from God. When you are weak, how do you turn to God to sustain you?

The second time, Satan tested Jesus' self-respect (spiritual pride) to which Jesus responds that he will not test the Lord. When have you purposefully placed yourself in a trying situation with an attitude that you cannot fail?

The third time, Satan offers Jesus power, prestige, and honor, to which Jesus responds that God holds the only place of honor for him. When are you tempted to seek approval from a certain group which you know will test your own convictions? Have you sought to solidify God's place in your heart?

Temptation is difficult to handle. In Jesus' case, his love for the Father, his nourishment from his relationship with the Father, and his humility not to test God enabled him to hold strong.

Take It to God

Pray that your relationship with God will be stronger and strive to nourish yourself on God's Word. Remain humble and know that you need to rely on God in everyday situations. Keep God as number one in all your relationships and you will find temptation less tempting and loyalty to God more appealing. Finally, pray at the times when you are weakest that God will strengthen you and keep you from trying situations.

Journal/Activity

With each of the three temptations above, you were asked for examples from your own life. Write down how you can respond differently to these types of situations in order to follow Jesus' example.

_____

_____

_____

_____

_____

_____

_____

_____

_____

_____

_____

_____

_____

_____

The Wrong Place at the Wrong Time

My Life

You may experience the most temptation of our culture in the area of sex. It is hard to avoid in the media and in every part of our society. But be honest with yourself: How often do you knowingly put yourself in this kind of tempting situation?

Setting the Scene

We find ourselves here in the middle of the Sermon on the Mount and Jesus is teaching us to pray. These famous words became part of what we now call the *Lord's Prayer* or the *Our Father*.

Matthew 6:13

Reflection

How often has a couple gone parking on a date or arranged their schedule to make sure they are alone where no one can disturb them and then participated in sexual activity that they later regretted? The real sin began when they purposefully set up the tempting situation in the first place.

We so often find ourselves in bad situations that we have created ourselves. We cheat on a test because we didn't study in the first place. We get upset about our assignment not being done on time, when we've waited until the last minute to do it. We get in a fight with Mom over a room not being cleaned when we put off doing it for three days. We constantly find ourselves in situations of stress and temptation because our own actions put us there.

"Lead us not into temptation" is a strange thing to ask God when we ourselves are fighting him by putting ourselves in those tempting situations.

The first step to resisting temptation is avoiding tempting situations. If you know your date and you are not exactly models of self control, don't park in a secluded spot. If you know you're tempted to cheat on a test, then study until you are confident enough to do the work on your own. If you and your Mom fight over your room, then clean it before she gets a chance to yell at you. Discipline your own actions and you won't have to be disciplined and you won't have to feel guilty. It's easier that way to stay loyal to yourself and to God.

Take It to God

Pray that God will give you the desire and the sense to avoid areas of temptation in your life. Pray the *Lord's Prayer* and listen to what you are asking for.

Journal/Activity

How about some good parent time? Share this reflection with a parent, especially those things which you promise to change in order to improve your relationship with them. You could even ask them if this reflection reminds them of situations in their life and how he/she got along with his/her Mom or Dad.

You Will Be What You Are Becoming

My Life

Have you ever looked at how you act and wished sometimes you acted differently, but it's hard to change?

Setting the Scene

Here in Pauls' letter to the Romans, Paul is trying to help the Romans deal with the same issue. He has just reflected upon the frustration of failing to act the way we want to, and he begins to talk about how we can change.

Romans 8:5-8

Reflection

I've never seen a good guitarist who hasn't played a lot of guitar. I haven't seen a great dancer who hasn't danced often. I've never seen a great student who hasn't studied many hours. Neither have I seen a holy person who hasn't prayed and done what is good, or a selfish person who hasn't lived for his own desires. You are a product of your life experiences to this point and what you will be in the future is dependent on what you will do today.

It only makes sense. You can't go to every keg party, hit all the R-rated movies, and put others down to bring up yourself, and turn out to be a neat Christian. These things form you just as reading Scripture, praying, and being kind to others forms you. The question is, What do you want to be?

One road leads to self-centeredness that can never bring you peace and the other to union with God and fulfilling what you were created to be. A little sin now leads to more later. A little good now can affect you just as much in the other direction.

If you water a plant, it grows. What you grow depends on what you plant. As long as you place yourself in situations where you will be tempted to sin, sin is condoned, and it abounds, that is what you will be. If you choose, instead, to surround yourself with situations in which open honesty, a sense of goodness, and respect of others and God abounds, then you will become one who seeks to do the same.

You're Worth It!

Take It to God

Pray for a clearness in your heart and mind about what you want. If what you want is a strong relationship with God and obedience to him, then pray that your friends and activities will enable you to grow in that direction.

Journal/Activity

Take a sheet of paper. Divide it into three columns. Label it at the top: good, bad, neutral. Try to recall as many circumstances/situations that you found yourself in over the last three months, including what you read and did. Enter each in the appropriate column. When you are done take a look at the columns. Determine what needs to change for you to continue to grow as a Christian.

_____

_____

_____

_____

_____

_____

_____

_____

_____

_____

_____

_____

_____

_____

_____

_____

No Strings Attached

My Life

Have you ever been in the position where you want two different things and you find it difficult to do both? You have to make a choice and that isn't always easy.

Setting the Scene

Here in Luke's Gospel Jesus has begun his public ministry. He has already recruited and prepared his 12 Apostles to help spread the Good News. Jesus now wants to expand and include others in changing the world around them, but in order to do so they have to make choices.

Luke 9:57-62

Reflection

A big stumbling block for many teens who want to follow Christ is dating a person who doesn't want to follow Christ. Dating the non-practicing Christian or non-believer can serve as a deterrent to the Christian and their willingness to follow Christ. Maybe you still go to church but being religious definitely doesn't fit in the relationship, which often leads to compromising with God.

One of the first things to do is go to the church youth group. That just isn't cool. When you lose the group you lose your peer support. That hurts because another reason for not following Christ is peer pressure. What our friends think of us is always important. Your closest friend is now a non-believer and your peer support is no longer your Christian friends. They may still be around but the closeness is tough to keep.

You have to decide if you really want to follow Christ. If you do, is it important enough to keep your relationship with God as the main priority in your life? If the answer is yes, you'll find the person you date will respect your desire for goodness more times than not. If the person does reject you because of your faith, then did that person really care about you? In dating a non-believer or having close friends who will not live a Christian life, sooner or later, they either change, learn to respect you, you change and compromise your relationship with Christ, or the friendships end. If they don't learn to respect your faith, they'll either reject you or force you to compromise. Can you respect yourself for that?

Take It to God

Pray that your dedication to Christ will have no strings attached. Pray for your friends who don't believe, that they may respect your faith and become open to God. Don't shove your faith down their throats. Nobody respects that. Keep your eyes fixed on Jesus, especially when you need a friend.

Journal/Activity

How do you see Jesus as a friend? Write down words of description that fit how you see Jesus. As you continue to reflect on Scripture your appreciation of the friendship Jesus offers you will grow.

_____

_____

_____

_____

_____

_____

_____

_____

_____

_____

_____

_____

_____

What Does God Ask of Me?

My Life

Just tell me what I need to do. Have you ever asked that question?

Setting the Scene

Micah was a prophet in Israel. Like many other prophets he spent his time calling the Israelites back to faithfulness to God. In this short passage you get in a nutshell the basic message he had to bring them.

Micah 6:8

Reflection

The prophet Micah followed the K.I.S.S. rule here. He kept it simple. We often complicate things and Micah keeps it simple for us. Micah wanted to let the Hebrew people know what God would have them do to make amends for their sins. "What sacrifice should we make?" the people asked. Micah responds with three simple things:

Do what is right. In almost any given situation we know what is right. The question is, Do we do it? It is harder than it sounds; we like to use excuses and get confused. When was the last time you convinced yourself it was okay to cheat on a test and then worried about being caught?

Love goodness. Is your heart divided? Is what is good that which appeals to you? We are all tempted by evil. Do you desire to have God give you a new heart? Do you work at forming proper values?

Walk humbly with your God. Are you the boastful type that walks with an air of cocky confidence? The super-Christian mentality leads us to not rely on God and to go on foolishly on our own. Do you continue to pray and seek God?

Take It to God

If you can learn to strive for these three actions you would please God. Pray that God will guide and strengthen you. Pray that God will continually renew your heart. Act according to what you know to be right and learn to love God's ways over what others tell you to do.

Journal/Activity

Write down specific points of conflict at school, with your friends, and at home where you feel uncertain and ask God to make clear to you the right thing to do. After that, follow your conscience.

_____

_____

_____

_____

_____

_____

_____

_____

_____

_____

_____

_____

_____

_____

_____

_____

_____

_____

_____

The Lighthouse in the Storm

My Life

Have you ever been lost and didn't know how to get back to familiar territory? Could you be lost in terms of relationships in your life or what you want to do in your future?

Setting the Scene

Back to the Sermon on the Mount. These two verses help summarize much of what Jesus had just said about how to get to what is really important in life.

Matthew 6:33-34

Reflection

When a ship is lost in a storm at sea, there's nothing more welcome than the bright rays of a lighthouse guiding it safely to shore. I'm sure as the captain of the ship nears land, he searches for that light as his hope for safety. Until the landing is secure, his attention does not waver from that light. Should that light diminish, the danger would unquestionably be heightened.

God is our lighthouse and he does not diminish. We, at times, keep our gaze fixed on God. But things can become distorted, and we can lose sight of the light and lose our direction. If life's journey, with all its unknowns, is going to have a sense of order, we must keep God as our focal point.

You have much of your life ahead of you; college or not college, new friends, new homes, moving out on your own. You may not be sure of what you want to do five years from now or what kind of person you'll be. God's promise is that if you keep God as your focal point, he will guide you, sustain you, and help you with all your needs. Live each day for God, and God will be with you with each day that follows.

Take It to God

Pray that God will remain number one in your life. Don't allow other things to become more important than God. He's the only lighthouse in the storm.

Journal/Activity

Reflect and write on these questions: What storms are in your life in which you lose sight of God? How do you fix your attention on God? What distracts you from following the light?

_____

_____

_____

_____

_____

_____

_____

_____

_____

_____

_____

_____

_____

_____

_____

_____

_____

_____

_____

_____

_____

God Reveals Himself to You

My Life

Have you ever found that if you spend enough time with someone, you get to know a little about them? You get to know your friends as you spend more time with them, doing things together. Under different circumstances you find out new things about them.

Setting the Scene

The Apostles here were getting reacquainted with their old friend, Jesus. It is shortly after the Resurrection and these Apostles still had not seen the Risen Lord.

Luke 24:30-35

Reflection

It is amazing to me how slowly they come to recognize Jesus, but as you read closely you can see that they were somehow restrained from recognizing him. Because of that, they were forced to get to know Him by what he revealed about himself. We get to know Jesus the same way. As we spend more time with him he reveals Himself to us and we get to understand him better.

The Apostles recognized Jesus in the breaking of the bread. There is a dual meaning here and both are good. One is the bread that represents our communion with God in the fellowship of the Christian community, and the other is the Eucharist that we share.

Take It to God

Pray that as you spend time with Jesus you may get to know him better and solidify your relationship with him and with your brothers and sisters in Christ.

Journal/Activity

Try to answer these questions: In the time you have spent with God, what has he revealed about himself to you? What has God revealed about you? How can you get to know God better?

But How Do I Pray?

My Life

Have you ever found it difficult to talk to God? Do you find it difficult because you don't know where to begin or what to say?

Setting the Scene

The followers of Christ had the same concern. Here, in the middle of his most famous sermon, the people asked Jesus to teach them to pray.

Matthew 6:9-13

Reflection

It's difficult to feel comfortable talking to someone that you can't see. I heard of someone who learned how to pray by talking to God on a phone. The most difficult part is to know what to say. A five-minute prayer can seem like an eternity. So here Jesus teaches his followers how to pray.

The prayer begins with us simply giving God praise. We're beginning with a welcome. When you speak with a friend, you don't ask them for something right away. You acknowledge them first. We do the same with God.

Second, we pray for God's will to be done. In whatever situation we come to God, no matter what the need, do we seek God's will or do we ask God to do ours? In seeking God's will in our prayers, we get to know him better and that is a key to prayer.

Third, we ask God to provide for our needs. Bring your personal problems to God. He wants to hear them. You bring your problems to your other friends. Bring them to God as well.

Fourth, we pray for forgiveness but only as we forgive. Think of those who have hurt you first and ask God to forgive them and to help you to do the same. The bitterness you release in doing that will bring you more peace sometimes than the forgiveness you receive yourself.

Finally, we pray that God will keep us from sin. Ask God to help you in those areas of your life in which you are weak. In this way you strengthen your relationship with God.

Take It to God

Say the *Lord's Prayer*, and with each part think of one area in your life to pray for that fits that part of the prayer.

Journal/Activity

Use this format to write your own prayer to God. Acknowledge God, pray for his will, bring him your needs, seek God's forgiveness, and ask him to strengthen you where you are weak and keep you from sin.

_____

_____

_____

_____

_____

_____

_____

_____

_____

_____

_____

_____

_____

_____

_____

_____

Learning to Listen to God

My Life

Do you find your life so full of what you need to do and what others want you to do that you can't find time to breathe?

Setting the Scene

Here in this passage we find the prophet Elijah on the run. He has done what God wanted him to do in proclaiming the truth to the queen, but she wanted him to agree with the other prophets who did not preach God's Word. Caught between conflicting expectations, and now fleeing for his life, Elijah hides out in a cave and waits for the Lord.

1 Kings 19:9-13

Reflection

The still voice of God is so difficult for us to distinguish. We live in a world of earthquakes, fire, and crashing rocks. Our life is so fast-paced and there is so much going on. Between school, sports, class plays, musicals, homework, church, home, jobs, family, friends, and our social life, we don't really find the time for listening to a still voice. When we do take the time to be with God, we bring with us all that is going on in our life. Our time with God is filled with thinking about any number of things that happened yesterday or will happen today. The distractions seem almost insurmountable.

Elijah, obviously, had his problems, too. The first thing God told Elijah to do is get away, and to find a place where he could be alone, and be able to listen to God. Elijah went off to the mountains, where God told him to go, and Elijah waited.

Where can you go? What place in your home, or at least close by, can you make special for your quiet time with God? The place should be one in which you won't be disturbed or distracted. The more regularly you go there, the more that place will help you to listen to God. Your mind will more and more drift toward God, and away from the hustle of everyday life. Have a quiet place for a quiet time, in order to listen to God's still voice.

Take It to God

Pray for God to help you discover a place and time where you can gather with him. Take enough time so you can clear your thoughts and focus on God. Dwell on things that pertain to God and soon you will learn to listen and hear God speaking in your heart, concerning his will and love for you. In experiencing this you will find great peace with God.

Journal/Activity

Spend five minutes alone with God. Get in a very comfortable position. Close your eyes. Take three or four very deep breaths and let each of them out slowly. Continue to breathe in a very relaxed pace. Be alone with God. Simply know that God is present with you and God will always be with you.

_____

_____

_____

_____

_____

_____

_____

_____

_____

_____

_____

_____

_____

The Purpose of God's Word

My Life

At this point it might be a little late to ask the question, but why should we read the Scriptures?

Setting the Scene

Here, in Paul's letter to the young disciple Timothy, Paul gives him much advice about being a young leader in the church.

2 Timothy 3:16-17

Reflection

There were two lovers separated by time and space and they longed to see one another again. What would the lover do who found out where the other was but had not the means to go to the other? That person would write a letter and in the letter she would share all that had happened since they were last together. She would express her love and how much she missed him. She would share how they could get together again. She would say where they would meet, and when and how to prepare to get there. She would seal the letter and mail it to him with the anticipation of seeing him again.

As soon as the loved one got his hands on the letter, he would open it and read its contents. He would follow the directions carefully until they were reunited.

That is the purpose of God's Word. It is a letter from our lover, God. In it God expresses his love for each of us. He provides a guide to live our lives, to believe in him with all our heart so that we may be with God forever. The Bible is God's Word. Like the letter, if we wish to know the directions to be one with God, we must read it, treasure it, and follow it.

Take It to God

Pray that God will give you an earnest desire to read his Word daily, that you may know God's will and be one with him.

Journal/Activity

Write a love letter to God. Tell God where you have been the last few months or years, what you need to do to get closer to him, and where you plan to pray each day.

You're Worth It!

Chapter III
Alienation within Family

Come to me, all you who labor and are burdened, and I will give you rest. Take my yoke upon you and learn from me, for I am meek and humble of heart; and you will find rest for yourselves. For my yoke is easy, and my burden light.

(Mt 11:28-30)

God Brings Order from Chaos

My Life

Have you ever felt like everything around you is going crazy and you feel totally stressed out? Even in your own home you may feel conflict and stress?

Setting the Scene

The creation story is not where the Scriptures begin. Exodus is believed to have been written first. The Israelites had already become a people. Like you and I, they had their questions, stresses, and concerns. Their faith in God is expressed in this story.

Genesis 1:1-5

Reflection

Today's family, in many instances, provides a sense of chaos that must have been similar to the beginnings of creation. Shortly after there were the heavens and the earth, there was the formless wasteland. When so many families today are torn by separation and divorce, parent-teen quarrels that can lead to running away, and constant moving because of jobs (which tears at a teen's foundation of friendships and peer security), it can seem reasonable for a young person to see their family structure as a wasteland.

In the case of divorce, sometimes you blame yourself, even though your parents assure you that you're not at fault (and you're not!). If you move often, you're afraid to make friends because it always hurts to leave them again. In all areas of conflict within families, the point is the same: the family, which should help bring a sense of order at a time in your life when there is so much changing in you, has instead heightened the level of change and brought a sense of chaos to your life.

Constant change in many areas of life brings on stress. At these times we need something constant. In the beginning, God brought order out of chaos. He organized time by day and night and brought order to the land and said it is good. He can bring order in your life as well, helping you to see that which is good.

Take It to God

In all your change, seek God who will be constant. Pray that your relationship with God will be stronger than ever as he helps you and your family members through their times of struggle. Give your family to God in prayer, that he may bring order into your lives. Put your trust in God for he will not change.

Journal/Activity

Make a list of the things in your life that haven't changed. Who is in your life today that was in your life a year ago? Include family, friends, relatives, etc. If you have moved away from anyone in the last year, write down other ways that you can keep them in your life. If you changed schools, what is similar about your new school compared to the old one? Write down other similarities in your neighborhood (malls, bowling, theaters, etc.) and in your church. Let this be your order as you accept changes in your life, and remember that through change we can grow and develop new friendships.

Don't Take Sides

My Life

Have you ever felt caught between two friends or two family members who were angry with each other?

Setting the Scene

Angels are God's messengers or representatives. Here an angel appears just before Joshua approaches the city of Jericho. It is shortly after the Israelites have entered the Promised Land and they are in constant conflict in trying to make their home there.

Joshua 5:13-15

Reflection

God does not take sides. He takes over. That is the case here in the Book of Joshua as he approaches the battle of Jericho. The angel of the Lord appears and claims neither to be against or for Joshua. In so doing, the angel has taken the side of truth. Even in the case of the Chosen People, where you would expect the angel to take sides, he does not. No matter how right anyone may appear, God does not take sides.

When we run into interpersonal conflicts within family, do we have a tendency to take sides? If Mom and Dad have a big fight do we run to the aid of one over the other? In this situation God runs to the aid of both.

This may not make sense at first, but in any given conflict seldom is one person totally right and one completely wrong. One thing is certain, though – both people probably hurt. In the case of your parents, it is something they need to work out. They may need professional help. That is not your job. You may feel the need to help. See a counselor at school or a priest or minister at church if you feel one of them is being abused. There may be a tendency to blame a parent or someone else. Blame doesn't help. Love does. Be an agent of love for both.

We don't need to solve the problem, but assure them of our love and understanding. There are times when a wrong is committed. We can be against the wrong but we must still love the person. Once we begin standing against the person we make it more difficult for relationships to heal. One final note: don't blame yourself for a conflict between two other people. It is their conflict. It affects you because of your love for both of them, but it is still their conflict to resolve.

Take It to God

It is not easy to be there and not take sides and still be supportive and caring for both. It's not easy to be against wrong but not against the person doing the wrong. Pray that God may give you guidance in loving both parties in an argument, whether it be brother and sister or Mom and Dad. God's guidance often comes through the gifts of others. If it is an ongoing conflict that is too difficult to bear or if it is abusive, God's guidance is there through a priest, minister, or counselor. Learn not to take sides and build resentments. Pray for those who are in conflict that God may heal their hurt and their relationship. Also, pray that God may heal the wounds that you may have because of the conflicts among those you love.

Journal/Activity

Conflict can be very hard on us. Sometimes we need someone to just listen. Write a letter to God and share how you feel about the conflict in your life. Don't hold any feelings back but dump them all on God.

_____

_____

_____

_____

_____

_____

_____

_____

_____

_____

Rebuilding Relationships

My Life

Are there relationships in your life where the walls between you are so high you don't know if they will ever come down?

Setting the Scene

After six days of marching around Jericho the Israelites were probably wondering how they were going to get by the actual walls they were facing.

Joshua 6:15-20

Reflection

The walls of Jericho stood between Joshua and the Israelites and victory. Through their obedience to God and acting on his instructions, the walls came tumbling down and they achieved victory. We, too, have walls in our lives which are barriers to victories in our relationships. We have walls within our homes. The question is, Where are the walls and how do we bring them down?

Walls can be built in any relationship starting with one bad experience or misunderstanding and not working it out. The feelings and resentments we feel continue to build up these walls until they seem insurmountable. Where have you built up walls and what are the building blocks of resentment? What can you do to bring down these walls and start to rebuild your relationships?

The first thing Joshua did was turn to the Lord for instructions. God's Word has so much to say about love and relationships. We find it easier at times to apply these principles to our neighbor than to apply them in our own home. If we want the walls to come down, we must learn to follow God's instructions in our home.

Take It to God

Act out of love. Pray for God's strength, for breaking down walls isn't easy. Pray for the ability to love. If there is a particular wall so old and large that you feel it can't be broken down, seek God's help possibly through counseling. All your walls must be broken down. The bitterness and resentment you carry from one relationship may hurt your growth in learning to love others.

Journal/Activity

Think of situations when you have failed in each of the following. Record how you failed and write down what you can do differently in order to tear down the wall and build a bridge instead. Do we listen to each other when we speak? Do we forgive when we've been wronged? Do we say, I'm sorry? Do we say, Thank you? Do we use positive statements to break down negative walls?

Identify the walls with your family members. Find their source and begin to make a change one step at a time.

_____

_____

_____

_____

_____

_____

_____

_____

_____

_____

_____

_____

_____

_____

_____

_____

Don't Carry the Load

My Life

Have you ever done anything that you feel is so bad you have never been able to forgive yourself?

Setting the Scene

As Jesus continues in his mission he reflects upon the work he has done and yet many do not reform their lives. He knows that for many the burden of change is too much.

Matthew 11:28-30

Reflection

Our greatest burdens are usually those we don't need to carry, but we refuse to give them up. We carry the burden of changing somebody we care for when only God changes hearts. We carry the burden of guilt for something we've done when Christ has already forgiven our sins. We carry the burden of relationships when relationships are meant to be shared. We carry our own sense of goodness and the responsibility for ourselves when Christ constantly calls us to allow him to be the master of our lives.

The result of carrying these burdens ourselves is that we give up because it's too much. We were never meant to change anybody, including those we live with. Nothing we have done wrong is greater than what God can do right, yet we continue to condemn ourselves for our sins. In all this we lose hope, but Jesus offers us some hope.

Jesus wants you to know that you don't need to carry guilt, just repent. He loves you too much to hold anything against you. Don't try and change people but rather let God, working through you, cause them to want to change. If you want people to love then be loving yourself, but let Christ be the source of your love.

Take It to God

Don't carry the burden yourself, but turn to Christ in prayer at every instance of need. Don't go it alone, but let God work and you rest in him.

You're Worth It!

Journal/Activity

On a separate sheet of paper write down the burdens that you carry no matter what they are. As a symbol of letting God help you to carry your burdens, crumple up the paper and throw it away. or burn the paper and let the rising smoke be a symbol of your giving your burdens to God.

_____

_____

_____

_____

_____

_____

_____

_____

_____

_____

_____

_____

_____

_____

_____

_____

_____

_____

Family Reunion

My Life

Do you have relationships in your life that you wish were close again? Do you have a sibling with whom you are constantly at odds?

Setting the Scene

Through the next five chapters of Genesis, the story of Joseph's life in Egypt leads to his place of power. If you have time to go back and read it, then do so. You will find how his brothers turned against him and it seemed they would never unite again. Examples of constant setbacks and eventual triumphs are told. Throughout these Scriptures, we see that God is at work in our lives.

Genesis 45:1-15

Reflection

The end result for Joseph is a reunion of love with his brothers and food in the midst of famine for his family. The greatest miracle for Joseph had to be his brothers' joy in seeing him. There was hatred before, but now there is love. Please note that it didn't come quickly. It took time to grow, there were experiences to learn from, and there was time to reflect.

Do you have a relationship in your family where it is difficult to share expressions of love? We all want love. We want relationships that foster it, and it hurts when our family relationships break down. It took time for them to break down. It will take time for them to heal. You will make progress and you will have setbacks, but don't lose hope. If the new foundation is to be strong, then it must be laid carefully. When the foundation is there, the reunion that comes about will be a moment to cherish.

Take It to God

Pray that God may give you patient endurance to be constant in love in order that healing may take place in your home. Restoration can take place, but all hearts must be open and that takes time.

Journal/Activity

Draw a picture of the foundation you need to build in order to build a loving relationship with the member of your family whom you need to grow closer to. If family relationships are great, think of a friend. In each brick of your foundation write a word that describes an attitude, characteristic, or quality upon which a loving relationship can be built.

How Do I Hang in There?

My Life

Have you ever been in the middle of something really important and you forgot why you were there? Why am I taking this class? Why did I want this job?

Setting the Scene

In this passage Jesus has sent the Apostles on ahead of him and later he comes out to join them as they drift in raging waters in the sea.

Matthew 14:25-30

Reflection

Keep your attention focused on Jesus. If Peter would have done that he wouldn't have faltered. He became distracted by the tossing waves and began to sink. You and I probably do the same thing. We haven't tried walking on water, but we have plenty of distractions in our lives, problems which distract us from keeping our eyes on Jesus. When we lose that focus our problems overtake us.

It wasn't over for Peter, for Jesus stretched out his hand and Peter was saved. Even when we do lack faith, we can still take Jesus' hand. All is not lost. Just like Peter, it is now time to reach out and take Jesus' hand. We can try walking on the water again, but this time keeping our focus on Jesus. We learn to do that a little better as we mature in Christ.

Take It to God

Pray that you will learn to focus on what Jesus would do in a situation. Keep him in mind when problems come about and let him be a reminder of how to work through your problems.

Journal/Activity

Try to answer these questions: What has happened in your family the last month that has caused you not to keep your focus on Christ?

What un-Christian characteristic in your attitude has been the result? What problem existed afterward because of your action? What will you do now that the problem exists?

_____

_____

_____

_____

_____

_____

_____

_____

_____

_____

_____

_____

_____

_____

_____

_____

_____

_____

_____

Reach Out

My Life

Have you ever lost a friend or family member? Whether because of death or because a friend has moved away, the grief or loss is hard to deal with.

Setting the Scene

In this passage, Jesus' friend Lazarus has died. As we begin this passage, Jesus is talking to Lazarus' sister Martha a few days after his death.

John 11:17-25, 39-44

Reflection

In one respect this passage isn't that consoling; after all, how often has God raised someone from the dead? In another respect it does say a lot. Martha found some comfort in Jesus' words that he was the Resurrection. She believes that Lazarus will go on living. The resurrection that follows serves to make a point that we may believe how real life is. We have in Lazarus tangible evidence of life after death.

For some of us, I still don't know how real that is. One thing we must learn in order to understand this spiritual life is to be active in that life now. The more alive we are in Christ, the easier it is for us to believe that life continues once we leave this earthly existence.

The part about the loss of a loved one is still difficult to deal with. Once we understand that they are with God, we still have the realization that they are not here with us. Believing that we will see them in heaven is great, but a part of us is missing. How do we fill the void of someone who means so much? The longer we dwell on their absence, the more difficult it is, yet we must accept their death before we can go on. And we must go on with the life God calls us to live.

First, now more than ever, develop a strong personal relationship with Christ. Jesus can do so much to heal our spiritual wounds. Learn to cry out to him. Learn to be angry with him. Learn to talk to him and rest in him. The help he gives you one-on-one cannot be replaced by others.

Second, reach out to others, both in seeking their friendship and offering yours. Give what you can to them and you will find you still have so much to give. The relationships you build in the process will enable you to stand strong and accept the loss of the relationship you had.

Rely on the communion of saints, both in the Church on earth and the Church in heaven, to pray for you. Don't forget that your loved one is still a part of that Church. As you pray for them, ask them to pray for you as well. Talk to them when you pray to the saints, to Mary, and to God. The relationship is different but it's there in a new way.

Take It to God

Pray that God may strengthen you and help you to deal with the flurry of emotions you will have. Experience each of them with God and with the support of your family and friends. God will be at your side as well as others who care.

Journal/Activity

Write a letter to a friend or family member who has died. If there is something that you wish you would have said to them before they died, say it to them now. Tell them how you feel about them. If there is something for which you need to say, "I'm sorry" or something to forgive, include that in your letter. At the end you may wish to end by promising to write again.

_____

_____

_____

_____

_____

_____

_____

_____

_____

My Purpose for Life

My Life

What is your purpose for life? Are you caught up in yourself or do you live serving others? Who gives you your reason for living each day? When you have lost a friend, what keeps you going?

Setting the Scene

We find Paul in prison contemplating the fact that he may be put to death. He reflects on the meaning of life and the purpose it gives him to live.

Philippians 1:20-26

Reflection

A student once asked me in jest what the meaning of life was. I'm sure I surprised him when I gave about a one-minute answer beginning with a quote from this passage. Christ means life. All life comes from him and through him was all life created. He provides the direction for all life and all life returns back to him. Outside of Christ there is no life, so the purpose of life can be found only in Christ. It is evident here as Paul debates the issue of where he would rather live — with Jesus in heaven or here on earth — that he grasped the meaning of life in Christ. Because of that understanding, he realizes that Gods' will is for us to live our lives fully here that others may come to know Christ.

If Jesus gives us our meaning in life, then our purpose for living will never leave us. Friends can move. Family members can die, but Jesus is always there. If we tie up our purpose in ourselves, our selfishness will stifle our sense of love and being loved. If our purpose is all caught up in others, excluding God, then we grow too dependent on someone whom we may lose. If we remain focused on Christ, he will enable us to love others, love ourselves, and go on living with a sense of purpose each day.

Take It to God

Pray that your relationship with Jesus will become more impor-

You're Worth It!

tant than any other relationship in your life. Have your purpose for existence be God, and you'll say with Paul that Christ means life, and you'll embrace life with joy and live it for all it's worth.

Journal/Activity

Using L.I.F.E. as an acronym, write four words beginning with those letters that represent what life means to you.

_____

_____

_____

_____

_____

_____

_____

_____

_____

_____

_____

_____

_____

_____

_____

_____

_____

_____

Moving On Again

My Life

How did you feel the last time you moved? Reflect back on a time when a friend moved away or you moved away from your friends.

Setting the Scene

This passage begins the call of Abram who was to become Abraham. The first thing God called him to do was to move away from his homeland in order to inherit what God had promised him.

Genesis 12:1-5

Reflection

Moving again! For some of us it becomes a way of life. Every two years Dad gets a promotion or gets transferred and we move. It's not easy. You just make new friends and now you have to say good-bye. It's getting to the point where you feel like it's better if you don't make any friends. It won't hurt as much when you move again and besides you feel you won't be around long enough to build a strong relationship anyway.

You are not the only one who feels that way. Moving can be tough. I heard one woman whose philosophy was quite good. Whenever they moved to a new place, the first thing she would do is contact her church and get involved in volunteer programs. She made a point of getting to know people. She made sure that the time spent in each place was meaningful and that she made new friends. As a result, she met more people and had more positive experiences.

Abram was called by God to constantly move. He had a reason. Abram was one day to become Abraham, the father of the Hebrew people. While on his journey, he passed through the Promised Land and gave thanks to God for it. He left his original home trusting that God had something better for him.

You can dwell on the negatives of moving or you can be like Abram or the woman mentioned above and emphasize the positive. What is good about each new place? What new friends can you make? What new experiences can you have? Abram didn't find the road easy, but

You're Worth It!

he did find it worth his effort.

Take It to God

Pray that God would help you to see the positive sides of moving. Be open to making new friends so that at each new place, you can experience newness in life and not withdraw from it.

Journal/Activity

Make a list of all the potentially good things that can happen to you in a new place, whether it be a new school or a new place to live.

_____

_____

_____

_____

_____

_____

_____

_____

_____

_____

_____

_____

_____

_____

_____

_____

God Is There Beside Me

My Life

Have you ever felt alone? You've lost a friend, you're mad at your family, or you've been cut from a team, and no one understands?

Setting the Scene

Jacob was one of Abraham's sons. Abraham wanted him to marry someone from his homeland so Jacob was sent off alone to find a wife. Jacob was now in, what was for him, a strange land with no one there beside him.

Genesis 28:13-15

Reflection

> An emptiness crept inside
> a soreness swells beneath my feet.
> I sit to rest from weariness
> there is God beside me.
> I sense God's presence when I go,
> He does not speak a word.
> I travel to an unknown place
> yet God is there beside me.
> A comfort it does give to know
> that though I travel far
> I will never be alone
> for God is there beside me.

God promised his presence to Abraham no matter where he would go and God promises to be with us as well. Be aware of God's presence. Take time with him and draw from his strength for wherever you go he is there beside you.

Take It to God

Pray for God's Spirit to bless you with a sense of his companionship as you live out todays' journey.

Journal/Activity

Take time in the quiet of the evening to take a walk. See in creation all the signs of God around you. Or think about a newborn baby you have seen recently. Each new life is a sign of God's presence.

_____

_____

_____

_____

_____

_____

_____

_____

_____

_____

_____

_____

_____

_____

_____

_____

_____

_____

_____

_____

My Parents Don't Understand Me!

My Life

Have you ever felt that no matter how hard you try you just can't seem to please your parents? You think you've done everything they've expected but they still don't appreciate you.

Setting the Scene

The prodigal son had just returned. He is the one who left with his inheritance and squandered it on sinful living. He realized his wrong and returned to his father sorry for his sin. While all this is going on the eldest son has done all that his father expected.

Luke 15:25-32

Reflection

Your parents don't understand you? That's true, but then who does? God does, but after him, perhaps you do not even understand yourself. You can expect parents to try to understand you and you can expect them to love you, but they won't always understand, and as long as you want them to understand you, you won't be satisfied. Personally, I would rather my parents loved me.

The brother of the prodigal son certainly felt his father was not sensitive to his feelings, nor was he fair. The prodigal son did every possible thing wrong, while the brother stayed home and did all that his father asked of him. I sympathize with the brother, yet at the same time, he's so hung up on a fair deal that he can't share the joy of his brother's return.

The father did not intend to take anything away from his eldest son. It was only to allow his youngest to know he was still loved. All he had will belong to the eldest. But when we're hurt there is much we can't see. We withdraw within ourselves. When have you been angry with your parents because of something they've done or said? When you grew angry, how did you respond to your parents? Did your anger cause you to resist whatever efforts they made to communicate?

Your parents won't understand you completely, nor did the father of the oldest son understand him completely. He did love him, though. He couldn't meet his need at that time, but down the road the elder son's needs will be met.

Take It to God

When you feel misunderstood, don't withdraw, but pray that God will enable you to control your emotions, so that you can still express your feelings. Don't expect understanding. Your parents are not God, but be thankful at any attempt they make to understand for this is a sign of their love for you.

Journal/Activity

Think of the last time you had a conflict with your parents where you felt they didn't understand you. Write down how you think they felt and what they wanted you to understand. Write down what you wanted them to understand about you. Set aside some time when you can share this with them. They will have an opportunity to understand you better and you will also have an opportunity to understand them.

_____

_____

_____

_____

_____

_____

_____

_____

_____

_____

_____

_____

_____

Healing after Rejection

My Life

Have you ever felt rejected by someone you love? That person's acceptance of you means a lot. There are times when you may feel rejection from your parents. It can be seen in different ways. They may stop listening to you or give up on disciplining you completely. The communication barrier builds. Maybe it's not common, but when it happens it hurts. It can mean not speaking to each other for a few days.

Setting the Scene

Stephen had reached out to his fellow Jews with the good news of God's love for them in Jesus. They did not understand or accept his message. Instead they were angry and their rejection led to violence.

Acts 7:54-60

Reflection

The Jews rejected Stephen to the point of stoning him to death. They did this because what he was saying went against the core of their innermost beliefs. When your foundation and your values are shaken, you feel anxious and you feel the need to shut out that which has hurt you. Many times a parent's rejection is preceded by a hurt they have received. Out of a sense of self-preservation they reject that which is a threat to them. It may not be your fault. It may not be something you did. They still love you.

Stephen's reaction was one of forgiveness. Yours must be as well, but it isn't easy. When it's only for a few days, then it's easy to talk out. Find out what you can do to help mend the wound and rebuild a stronger relationship. When the conflict lasts over a long period of time, then don't rush it. Your parents may not be ready. Seek out counseling, especially if the rejection means you're not living at home, because you need help in dealing with your feelings. The rejection has wounded you and your self-image.

Take It to God

Pray for God to help you to see all that is good in you. Pray for your parents and pray for God to help you to forgive them. Deal with your shortcomings and theirs one at a time. Be patient and be ready to rebuild the relationship with your parents slowly.

Journal/Activity

Feeling rejected hurts. Spend some time with a friend who accepts you for who you are. Share your hurt. Ask them to share with you the things about you that they treasure.

God's Child by Adoption

My Life

What images come to mind when you think of God? Does God seem close or distant, loving or judgmental?

Setting the Scene

Here in the eighth chapter of Paul's letter to the Romans, Paul reflects on a series of reasons why we cannot be separated from the love of God. One reason is how God sees us.

Romans 8:14-17

Reflection

Abba! In the New Testament, this word means "father." It is not a formal way to address God, but a term of endearment. I believe within the context of our society it would be more appropriately translated as Dad. Can you imagine starting you prayers to God with Dad? It almost sounds insulting to some, but I think it is beautiful.

When my father died when I was 12, I began my informal prayer life. Up until then it was all memorized prayer. I would ask God if I could talk to Dad. I would wait, as if he said "yes," then begin talking to my father. I would share with him my day and ask how everything was up in heaven. I'll never forget it. I loved him so much and those times of prayer meant a lot to me because he was Dad. I would say good-night and thank God for letting me talk to him.

God is my heavenly Dad. Knowing that God is your Dad can mean a lot when you are dealing with rejection. He adopted us. Jesus is our brother and we'll always be together. He went through a lot to adopt us, much as parents who adopt their children do today. It's a tremendous act of love, to choose a specific person and say, "I love you." If you are adopted, know that you were chosen to be loved by your adoptive parents. Also know that all of us are adopted by God and that God freely loves us and always will.

If you have felt rejection from your earthly parents, know that you have a heavenly parent who never rejects you and always loves you. He will be there to help you through, as you and your earthly parents reconcile.

Take It to God

Pray today and call God Dad. Start sharing your day with him with all its problems and successes. Begin developing intimacy with your adoptive heavenly father, God, and your adoptive brother, Jesus. Ask God to fill you with his Spirit.

Journal/Activity

Write a letter to God about anything that is on your mind. Begin with Dear Dad and refer to God as Dad throughout your letter.

_____

_____

_____

_____

_____

_____

_____

_____

_____

_____

_____

_____

_____

_____

_____

_____

_____

My Parents Are, Too

My Life

Are there times when being around your parents is a source of irritation? Why do you think it is that there are times that no matter what your parents say, you feel on edge?

Setting the Scene

Back to Jesus' most famous sermon, the Sermon on the Mount. In this passage we have a collection of the main substance of all of Jesus' teachings. In it we find a blueprint for life.

Matthew 7:1-5

Reflection

We become so concerned about our growth and our rights that we forget that our parents are growing, too. They, too, are adopted children of God. We forget that. We're probably harder on our parents than on anyone else. We constantly judge them. Sounds a bit strange, but think about it. Our friends and our parents could say the same thing, but with our friends we'll accept it, with Mom and Dad we'll say they're on our back again. We might seem on edge around them and when they make a mistake, especially in parenting, it's bigger than life.

How do you judge your parents?
Are you at times shocked when you find out that they've done something you consider wrong?
When you feel they're making a mistake as a parent, do you resent them?
Do you think you're going to be a perfect parent?
Do you pray for them that they may grow?
Are you concerned with their happiness and well-being?

With all these questions, does your mood at the time affect your answer? If it does, then you know that they and you are both in need of growth. Their moods sometimes affect their response to you, too.

Take It to God

Pray that God will give you a nonjudgmental attitude toward Mom and Dad. Pray that you will become concerned with their feelings and well-being. Recognize that they are growing and they are children of God, too.

Journal/Activity

Imagine yourself as a parent with all the various responsibilities you will have. Imagine your teenager coming to you with some of the same issues you now bring to your parent(s). Write out a role play on how you think it will go.

_____

_____

_____

_____

_____

_____

_____

_____

_____

_____

_____

_____

_____

_____

_____

_____

_____

I'm Getting Older, Mom and Dad

My Life

Do you sometimes feel like your parents treat you like they did four years ago? You feel you're more responsible but they haven't got a clue.

Setting the Scene

Mary, Joseph, and Jesus have just concluded their pilgrimage to Jerusalem. Jesus was 12 years old and had reached the age of adulthood in ancient times. As they traveled in those times, it would be possible to have traveled a great distance before realizing someone was missing.

Luke 2:48-52

Reflection

Jesus grew more quickly than anyone would have thought. His wisdom was beyond his years so he went off in the temple pursuing his vocation in life at an early age. His parents, on the other hand, were rightfully concerned for him and upon finding Jesus, proceeded to bring him home. They did not understand him. They saw a boy and he was becoming a man.

Do you feel that frustration at times? You want to announce to your parents that you are getting older. You're not a little girl or little boy anymore. In a few years you'll vote and maybe you already do. You can get a job. You're smarter than they think. At this point thoughts of rebellion seep in. You feel your parents are holding you back so you might sneak around to do the things they have forbidden you to do.

Jesus was obedient to his parents. If anyone had the right to say, "Mom and Dad you're holding me back," it had to be Jesus, the Son of God. He didn't. He recognized the role of his parents. He continued to grow and mature at home. Sure, there was much he could do, but he wasn't done growing yet and neither are you.

It's tough at times not to sneak away, but that's not going to convince Mom and Dad of your maturity. They have to see it themselves, and your own sense of responsibility will reveal your growth to them.

Mary thought about what happened that day. Parents usually do.

Take It to God

Pray that God will help you not to rush your growth. You have a lot of years ahead of you. Dwell on the attitude of Jesus in this case and seek to have his attitude be yours.

Journal/Activity

What do you think the conversation between Jesus and Mary was like? Write out how you think the conversation went. What do you learn from looking at what Jesus would say and what he did in his situation?

Making New Beginnings

My Life

Think of a time when you were given a new opportunity to prove yourself. Did you retake a test that you failed? Did you try out for a new team? Were you ungrounded and allowed to go out again?

Setting the Scene

Jesus told many parables to help people understand what living for him would be like. He tried to help them see that there was something new and exciting about the Good News he brought them.

Mark 4:30-34

Reflection

The mustard seed is the perfect analogy for anything that starts with small beginnings and is to become something beautiful. It is used here to symbolize the Kingdom of God. If you look at its development you'll find how Jesus, planting a seed of faith in a small group of men and women, began a Church that would spread his Kingdom throughout the earth for thousands of years. The Kingdom will last forever.

We need mustard seeds in our relationships with our parents, too! All you need is a mustard seed. Your seed need only be the fact that you want a fresh beginning. God's Word will provide you with many of the tools to help the relationship grow. That seed must be nurtured and must be planted with faith.

The nurturing will come from your reliance on God to help your heart be fertile soil for change. Be open to God's word and allow the Spirit to work within you. You're worth it and so are your parents.

Take It to God

Pray that God will grant you the faith of a mustard seed that you may believe in a stronger relationship with your parents. Don't settle for anything less than a relationship where love is the key characteristic. With God nurturing that seed, it will grow to be a beautiful plant.

You're Worth It!

Journal/Activity

Get a small pot and place some dirt in it. Get a seed for any small flower. Plant it, water it, and nurture its growth. Let the symbol of the growing plant be a sign of how you must plant seeds of respect and love and nurture those seeds so they can grow and benefit your relationships in your family.

_____

_____

_____

_____

_____

_____

_____

_____

_____

_____

_____

_____

_____

_____

_____

_____

_____

_____

_____

_____

_____

_____

Learning to Listen

My Life

Have you ever rushed into to doing the right thing only to find that you didn't know what was expected of you?

Setting the Scene

Martha and Mary were sisters of Lazarus. They were among Jesus' closest friends. This type of visit was probably not unusual.

Luke 10:38-42

Reflection

No, this doesn't mean you don't have to do your housework. Sorry. Not all is lost, though, for contained in Mary's example is a great lesson for building a relationship with anyone. Listening is a key to the communication necessary for a good relationship. Martha and Mary give us great contrast in how it is done.

Martha is present to Jesus much the way we are to each other. We do anything but sit down and listen. How often have you listened to your parents while watching TV or listening to music with headphones on? When around each other we busy ourselves with so many distractions that we don't get to know each other.

Mary, on the other hand, puts aside what she could be doing and listens to Jesus, with her whole attention focused on him. She doesn't just hear his words, but she listens to what he is saying. When was the last time you sat down and had a good talk with one of your parents? Are you really getting to know each other or are you becoming strangers?

You can't expect a good relationship if you don't know Mom and Dad, or if they don't know you. Spend time with them. Ask them how their day went and really listen. Care about them and show it.

Take It to God

Pray that God may give you opportunities to be with each other and when those opportunities come – listen.

Journal/Activity

Take one of your parents out to lunch without any agenda of your own. Ask them questions about their work and their hopes and simply listen.

Love Is the Key

My Life

What does the word love mean to you? Think of the times you have used that word in the past few days.

Setting the Scene

This classic passage to the Corinthians falls in the midst of several passages in which Paul is talking to the Corinthians about how they are to live together as a community. They have not always gotten along. They bicker a lot. In the midst of this Paul speaks.

11 Corinthians 13:4-7

Reflection

We so quickly use the word "love" that it begins to lose its meaning. "I love hot dogs" and "I love my friends" certainly carry quite different meanings, yet "love" is the same word. So what do we mean when we say, "We love our parents"?

This passage defines love for us. Compare your relationship with Mom and Dad to this passage and find out how effectively you love. One way of doing so is to reread the passage replacing the word love with your name ... John is patient, John is kind and continue until you have read the whole passage.

How accurate was that passage this time? Where do you feel you fail to love?

In what instance were you strongest? In what circumstance with your parents have you failed to love?

Take It to God

Pray that God will give you the discipline to work on each area of your ability to love.

Journal/Activity

Make a list of those virtues that are weakest in you. Ask God to help you in each instance. This passage is challenging, but you have here a detailed account which will enable you to measure your love and become a more loving person. That's exciting. This is the key for a stronger relationship with anyone, including Mom and Dad.

_____

_____

_____

_____

_____

_____

_____

_____

_____

_____

_____

_____

_____

_____

_____

_____

_____

_____

_____

_____

_____

The Power of the Tongue

My Life

When you look at the conversations between you and your parents, how often do you say kind things?

Setting the Scene

The Book of Proverbs contains a collection of many wise sayings for living. Many of them are attributed to Solomon, the third king of Israel, known for his wisdom.

Proverbs 10:14

Reflection

My father used to tell us if we didn't have something good to say to someone, then don't say anything at all. How often have you said something without thinking and really hurt someone or had that happen to you? On the other hand when you have really worked hard at something a kind word can mean so much.

For many parent-teen relationships, the majority of conversations revolve around disagreements. As a result the relationship is built more on negative remarks than positive statements. What kind of relationship are you left with?

Begin today to think of things that your parents are working on or doing that mean a lot to them. What positive statements can you make? Tell Mom she cooks a great meal. Thank Dad for picking you up after school or taking you to school events. Never forget Mother's Day or Father's Day! They may say you don't need to remember, but deep down saying "I love you" always means a lot.

Take It to God

Know the power of the tongue. It can build up and it can tear down. Allow love to be its guiding force and ask God to teach you self-control.

Journal/Activity

Make a list of the last ten conversations you had with one of your parents. What kind words were spoken? What unkind words were spoken? How many times was the conversation about a problem? Now write down ten things your parent(s) do. Think of one kind thing you can say about each and make sure you communicate the kindness over the next week. Take time now to thank God for the kind things your parents do for you.

A Parent Who Cares

My Life

Sometimes a parent's response to your perceived inappropriate behavior can be tough. Have you ever resented the discipline your parents have handed out? Do you think they are too strict?

Setting the Scene

Discipline from parents during the time of this writing was probably stricter than it is today. In this letter to a young community of believers in Rome, the author tries to help the young disciples to see the difficulties of living the Christian life in an un-Christian land in a different light.

Hebrews 12:5-6

Reflection

According to this passage not only does the Lord discipline, but the thought of it is supposed to be encouraging to believers. It is encouraging because discipline is a sign of love. Certainly if this is true with God then it must be true for parents as well.

Parents who cease to discipline should be more of a concern than those who discipline too much. I'm not suggesting any particular form or amount of discipline for a given situation. A parent should never be physically or emotionally abusive. I am suggesting that a parent who loves you will be actively concerned with what you do and what influences your growth. A Christian parent will be concerned with the values you form and the manner in which they are expressed.

How would you feel if your parents didn't care about what kind of person you are or what kind of person you will become? Would you be convinced they cared? Perhaps their manner of discipline is not to your liking, but someday your kids will question you when you discipline them as well.

Take It to God

Be thankful for the signs of love shown through the discipline of your parents. Pray that Gods' wisdom will guide their decisions as well as your growth. They are a means by which God will form you. Recognize that their discipline won't always be perfect but it should always be done with your best interest in mind and with love. Trust that the result in the end will be your well-being and that you will continue to grow into the image of God.

Journal/Activity

It's not uncommon for teens to say to themselves, "I'll never do that to my children." Write down the things your parent(s) do when they discipline you that you do want to repeat with your own children someday.

_____

_____

_____

_____

_____

_____

_____

_____

_____

_____

_____

_____

_____

_____

_____

A Good Philosophy toward Parents

My Life

Who have you been able to talk with about your problems (not including someone like a counselor or priest)? Are there people in your life with whom you feel you can be open and tell very personal things?

Setting the Scene

For many, this single verse in the Sermon on the Mount captures the heart of the sermon's message—the Golden Rule.

Matthew 7:12

Reflection

How would you describe the person to whom you turn when you are in need? Does he or she put you down or do you feel accepted by them? Are they always talking or do they also listen? Are they there for problems only or do they consider you a friend? Most likely the person with whom you can share your intimate self is a person with whom you feel accepted, who will listen to you, and will be there for you. That person demands respect because of who he or she is.

Many times we wish we could have that kind of relationship with our parents. The truth is, many parents would like to have that same kind of relationship with their kids. If we look at those with whom we do share, we can learn a lot about building that kind of relationship with our parents.

If you want to be listened to, you must learn to listen. If you want to be accepted, you must accept them. You must learn the Golden Rule of doing unto others as you would have them do unto you. As this sums up the law of the prophets so it also sums up the attitude we need to have toward our parents if we wish for respect.

Do you accept your parents for who they are or do you want them to fit your image of what a parent should be? Do you listen to them as they express their feelings? Do you help them to feel good about who they are?

Take It to God

Pray that God will give you an attitude of understanding toward your parents. Pray that the spirit of the Golden Rule will become a more natural way of relating to your parents as you begin each new day with them.

Journal/Activity

Make a list of the things you would want your children to do unto you if you were a parent. Pick one that you need to start doing for your parent(s).

_____

_____

_____

_____

_____

_____

_____

_____

_____

_____

_____

_____

_____

_____

_____

_____

Authority

My Life

Have you ever done something just because you were told not to or not done something because you were told to do it?

Setting the Scene

In this prophetic parable of the Old Testament, Jonah is asked to preach repentance to Israel's greatest enemy of that time. Jonah had no interest in seeing them repent; rather, he wanted them to experience God's wrath.

Jonah 1:1-3, 10-12

Reflection

I'll bet when Jonah found himself in the midst of the storm he began to wonder if he made the right choice. Maybe God wasn't asking too much? All He asked him to do was preach. When we're asked to do something it seems so burdensome. When we run from responsibility we find, at times, that running has a price,

Sometimes you just don't want to obey. The reasons vary, but there are times when reason has nothing to do with it. We just don't feel like it. Add any reason or excuse on top of that and there's no changing our mind. Parents ask you to do many things, but how much is it compared to the price that you pay for disobeying?

What is the price? What kind of relationship do you have with Mom and Dad when you refuse to do what they tell you? What kind of anxiety do you create for them and for yourself? Do you feel they ask too much? What's fair? Jonah thought God was asking too much. Was he better off running away?

You are heading toward a time when you have to become responsible for your life. Some parents may be slow in allowing you to experience enough freedom to grow up, but the cost of rebellion or running is too great. There are also many times that they may be right. When they are wrong, your own sense of responsibility will show them. Also, the trust you build by obeying will enable them to give you more freedom.

Take It to God

Pray that you may have an open mind to the value of authority in your life. Pray that as you appreciate that value you will retain the ability to ask questions and to learn the reasons why.

Journal/Activity

Think of another authority figure in your life like a coach or teacher. Compare how you respond to their authority versus how you respond to your parents. Who do you show more respect for? What are the consequences?

Maybe They Had a Point

My Life

Have you ever tried something you didn't want to try only to find out that it was a lot better than you thought it would be?

Setting the Scene

After a great deal of resistance Jonah finally preached God's message to the Ninevites. The great city of the Assyrians had heard the word and, led by their king, repented.

Jonah 3:6-10

Reflection

"He likes it! Hey Mikey!®" is a well-known line of an older brother in an old Life® cereal commercial. The cereal that Mom said was good for the boys in the commercial obviously couldn't be good, so the older brother had his human guinea pig, Mikey, try it out. Low and behold, it tasted good. Mom turned out to be right, but without Mikey who would have known?

As a teen, doing something because Mom and Dad said so isn't cool. We want to strike out on our own and learn for ourselves, but along the way we, to some degree, discredit our parents' opinion. They still might know a thing or two and it might pay to at least listen. Jonah struck out on his own, stumbled, and then God rescued him. Then he gave God's idea a shot and, would you believe it, it worked. The people of Ninevah repented and were spared destruction.

God had a point to make. He's not the only one. Sometimes you have a point to make and when people, including parents, don't listen, you can get angry. Parents experience the same frustration when we don't allow them to make their point and respect their experience and authority.

Has your relationship with them broken down to the point where you automatically do the opposite whenever they tell you what to do in a particular situation? "Mikey" would have never known how good the cereal was unless he tried it.

Take It to God

Pray that you may become more open to listen to your parents and consider their point of view.

Journal/Activity

Pick one area of direction your parents have given you and you have refused to cooperate in; start doing it/cooperating. Watch over the next few days and see how it affects your relationship with them.

_____

_____

_____

_____

_____

_____

_____

_____

_____

_____

_____

_____

_____

_____

_____

Learning the Easy Way

My Life

Can you think of a time in your life when you were too stubborn to listen and you had to learn the hard way? Maybe you refused to do your homework and you flunked a course. Maybe you refused to practice and you were cut from a team.

Setting the Scene

At the end of the journey, Jonah now sits angry because God let Nineveh off the hook. Jonah just doesn't understand why God didn't destroy them. God tries one more time to get Jonah to understand.

Jonah 4:5-11

Reflection

After the initial refusal to obey, being saved from the large fish, and success met through obedience, Jonah still didn't learn. He was still stuck on his own way. God allows one final illustration to make his point. Hopefully, Jonah learned something about God's love. More important, I hope he learned his lesson concerning his relationship with God and learning the easy way.

Often, learning by our mistakes can leave an impression that makes the lesson memorable. We sit back and say that experience is the better teacher. That is valid, but along with our own experience, there is the collective experience of those who went before us. If the only way to learn was by our own experience, then learning not to walk in front of a speeding truck would leave a lasting impression on all of us, one at a time.

As we head toward our adult life, the human experiences we have can be more rewarding as well as more damaging. We need guidance so that our experiences may teach us, without leaving permanent damage. When the risks are higher, take more caution. Your parents may, at times, cause you to step out more slowly than necessary, but your tendency will be more to run when you should walk. There will be a tension, but the balance will help you to grow.

Take It to God

Some lessons, if learned the hard way, will cause you to regress rather than proceed. Pray for the wisdom to know the difference. Listen to the experience of those who went before you. Know that even though they may be overcautious, your parents' motivation in giving you advice is more likely to be in your best interest.

Journal/Activity

Recall and write down one experience in which you didn't listen to someone's advice and later wished you did.

_____

_____

_____

_____

_____

_____

_____

_____

_____

_____

_____

_____

_____

_____

_____

_____

What Should I Be Thankful For?

My Life

Have you ever known someone who never said thank you no matter how nice you were to them?

Setting the Scene

The Psalms are full of all kinds of writing, including hymns of sorrow, prayers of petition in time of need, hymns of thanksgiving for what God has done, and hymns simply worshiping God. Here the psalmist writes a hymn of thanksgiving to our God.

Psalm 100

Reflection

A pessimist would look at a sunny day and say that it will probably rain tomorrow, while an optimist would look at a rainy day and thank God that the flowers will grow and tomorrow will bring sunshine. You can look at all your struggles and see problems or look at them and see opportunities for growth. How we look at our lives has as much to do with our emotional well-being as the situations in which we find ourselves.

Psalm 100 is a song of praise recognizing that ultimately we are God's children and we should give him thanks. For what have you thanked your parents? Let's go through a checklist and see what we should be thankful for.

Have you thanked God for your parents giving you life?

Have you thanked God that your parents gave up so much freedom in order to have you?

Have you considered what your parents had to give up to have you?

Have you thanked God for the times Mom or Dad stayed with you when you were sick?

How many times have your parents taken you and your friends where you wanted to go?

How often have your birthdays been special?

How many meals have been prepared for you over the course of one year?

How often have your clothes been washed?
Do you think it's fun to change diapers?
In your lifetime, how often have you heard "I love you"?
How many hugs have you had?
Have you thanked God that your parents still worry?
Have you thanked God that they still care where you go?

Take It to God

The list could go on indefinitely. What do you have to be thankful for? Make a list and thank God for each item on the list and then share your gratitude with Mom and Dad. Then, believe me, they will feel cause to be thankful too.

Journal/Activity

Make a list of everything your parents do for you. Write a thank you note to them for all that they do and leave it for them in a place where you know they will find it.

Chapter IV
Alienation from Friends

Love is patient, love is kind. It is not jealous, love is not pompous, it is not inflated, it is not rude, it does not seek its own interests, it is not quick-tempered, it does not brood over injury, it does not rejoice over wrongdoing but rejoices with the truth. It bears all things, believes all things, hopes all things, endures all things. Love never fails. (1 Cor 13:4-7)

Building Friendships

My Life

Do you find that when you want something in your life you want it now? We live in a world of instant gratification with fast food restaurants, computers, air travel, and television, and we also seem to desire instant friendship. We could be new in a neighborhood or school, or just find ourselves temporarily in a new situation, like a summer cottage. We all feel the need for an instant friend. Some-times it works, but sometimes we get hurt.

Setting the Scene

We find ourselves here at the scene of Jesus' last night with the friends he has made and spent time with for the last three years. It is his last supper. Tomorrow he will be arrested.

Matthew 26:21-35

Reflection

Friendship takes time to develop and we invest in it a little at a time. We need someone we can trust. We need someone we can trust with our inner self, but that person must prove trustworthy as we need to be trustworthy for them. Knowing each other takes time. Each of us is complex with a mixture of values, emotions, and beliefs. It takes time to burrow through the masks we wear to find the real person. Many of us wear masks for the sake of acceptance. When the mask drops then we will know the person and true friendship can begin. At that time we can be accepted for who we really are, which is the basis of true friendship. In this passage it is clear that Jesus knows his friends after three years. He knows who will let Him down, who will betray Him and who will stand by His side.

If you need friendship then be a friend. Be honest about who you are. If you don't wear a mask, it's true that not everyone will accept you, but those who do will accept you for who you are. They'll feel more secure in being themselves. You'll get to know each other more quickly and true friendship will take place.

Take It to God

Pray that God will give you the courage to be the person you are. He made you and He knows you better than anyone else does. Pray for patience, so that you can allow friendships to develop without pushing it and without masks. Pray for God's comfort for the times you found out that someone you thought was a friend turned out not to be one.

Journal/Activity

Describe what you look for in a true friend. Pick out the characteristics you most admire and strive to the best of your ability to practice those virtues yourself.

Betrayed Me with a Kiss

My Life

Have you ever been betrayed by someone who has been your friend for a long time? After years of being a good friend to them you may find out that they aren't what you thought they were.

Setting the Scene

It is now after the Last Supper. Jesus has prayed in the garden. His friend of three years, Judas, now approaches Him surrounded by guards with weapons.

Luke 22:47-53

Reflection

Betrayed Me with a Kiss

We walked the streets of Jerusalem
and shared the same cup of wine.
We sailed the Sea of Galilee,
reaching out to the poor and the blind.
Three years of touching other's hearts
as ours grew stronger each day,
mine towards this day of sacrifice,
but his strayed another way.
I knew this time was coming.
His embrace would bring my end.
Swords and torches swirl around me,
in their midst stands my trusted friend.
With his eyes fixed firmly on me,
with a sorrow I could not miss,
I said "Friend, do what you must do."
and he betrayed me with a kiss.

Calling Judas friend at that time of betrayal says so much about Jesus' capacity to love. If only Judas would have seen the forgiveness, but he didn't. I don't know how any of us could have understood what was going on in Jesus' mind. Perhaps to some extent we can empathize if we have ever felt betrayed. I doubt if any betrayal could be so complete as this, yet Jesus could still be a friend.

Take It to God

When you feel betrayed by a friend, turn to Jesus. Ask Him for His comfort and healing. Pray that Jesus would give you the strength to remain who you are as he did. Know that in your hurt there is One who understands.

Journal/Activity

Place yourself at Jesus' side after he was betrayed by Judas. Write down your imagined conversation with Jesus thinking of what you would say to him and what he would say in return.

_____

_____

_____

_____

_____

_____

_____

_____

_____

_____

_____

_____

_____

_____

_____

Good Outweighs the Bad

My Life

Have you ever lost a friendship because of one incident? All the good that the relationship held, the good times over the months and years must end because we can't say "I'm sorry" or "I forgive you"?

Setting the Scene

The psalmist in his prayer reflects upon the lack of faithfulness of those around him but realizes who his faithful friend is.

Psalm 12

Reflection

Have you ever felt like the psalmist with your friends? They may have been your friends for years but now you have heard they are talking behind your back. Is the anger we hold so precious that we give up the friendship we had? Sometimes we convince ourselves that the answer is "yes" as we judge the intent of our friend's actions and do not take into account the good intent of the acts of friendship they've shown in the past.

When a good friend says or does something that hurts, the wound is deeper than if it comes from someone who isn't a close friend. We have opened up more of ourselves so naturally we are vulnerable to greater injury. At the time of the hurt the rewards of the open relationship don't seem worth the cost.

Stop and ask yourself a few questions:

How does resentment make you feel?
Have you ever let someone down?
If not, have you ever let God down?
Does God hold a grudge against you?
Can you afford to hold a grudge against a friend?

Take It to God

Pray that God may enable you to bear your hurt, not hold a grudge, and openly tell your friend how you feel. Ask God to help you to remember what is good and not dwell on the singular bad occasion.

Journal/Activity

List all the good times you have had and the things you've shared. Does the good outweigh the bad? If you have had a true friendship, then the good will outweigh the bad.

Keep it between the Two of You

My Life

Have you ever been hurt by what one person said about you to others? The rumor spread and gets back to you and you're really hurt?

Setting the Scene

In Chapter 18 of Matthew's Gospel we find a series of teachings and stories from Jesus that help us with relationships, with a key emphasis on mercy and understanding.

Matthew 18:15-18

Reflection

There was a shampoo commercial years ago where one girl told two friends about this great shampoo and they told two friends and so on until everybody knew. I've seen people handle other people's problems the same way. It may be good for shampoo but not for friendship, and especially when someone tells you something personal. Good seldom comes from sharing a conflict in relationships with another friend, especially if the friend is mutual. For some reason what is told to a few in confidence becomes the latest gossip on the grapevine.

I've had people come to me from both sides of a conflict and I've tried to encourage them to talk to each other, to share the same thing they told me with the person with whom they have the problem. The sooner they can talk to each other the sooner the problem is resolved; when the meeting is delayed, however, the need to share the burden draws more people into the mix.

Interpersonal relationship problems become complex because feelings are complex. When we draw in more people we draw in the complexity of all their feelings. Whatever good we accomplish in the way of advice is often offset by the division that arises among all the friends who become involved. Try and work it out between the two of you.

If you need advice in dealing with a serious problem, seek out someone who is either not a mutual friend or someone who is older. Maybe someone at your church can be of help or an older brother of sister. Share only what you're struggling with and not the other person's private concerns. Gather what guidance you need in order to go directly to the person and then go to them.

Take It to God

Pray through all this that God will give you words to say, a loving heart, and a spirit of forgiveness. Only seek the help of another person if you can't handle the situation yourself and leave all mutual friends out of it. If you leave it between the two of you then only the two of you will have a problem.

Journal/Activity

During the coming week don't repeat one word that anyone says about another person. If the other person needs to know, then encourage the person who is doing the talking to go to the person instead of talking about them.

_____

_____

_____

_____

_____

_____

_____

_____

_____

_____

_____

_____

Be Thankful for What You Have

My Life

Have you ever felt resentment of someone else because you were jealous of them? They didn't do anything to harm you but you just don't like them?

Setting the Scene

Contained in these chapters of Genesis is the story of Joseph and his 11 brothers. Joseph was the favorite son of his father and the others were jealous of the affection Joseph received.

Genesis 37:3-4

Reflection

In I Corinthians 13, jealousy is listed as one of those vices that is opposed to love. Here, in this passage, we see jealousy maturing into hatred, which would seem to be its natural course. Joseph didn't seem to understand the nature of jealousy. If you read through the chapters of Genesis, which contain his story, you will find that he flaunted the favoritism his father had for him. This only caused the brothers to grow more jealous, and thus we have the hatred that later led them to get rid of Joseph.

Jealousy in your relationships can have the same effect if you allow it to grow. Love is centered on others. It wants what is best for them. When jealousy surfaces, its concern is not caught up in being happy for the other person, but wanting what they have for the self. Jealousy is selfish. Because of its selfish nature it tears down relationships.

Of whom have you been jealous? What effect has your jealousy had on the relationship? Have others been jealous of you? Have you flaunted something that others were jealous of?

Take It to God

If something someone else has is worth having, learn to be thankful for what you have and be happy for them at the same time. If it is a gift or ability, then pray to God. You may also have that gift and only need to see it in others so that it may be drawn out of you. Above all, pray that love would be the key to your relationships. As long as concern for others and love for self is firmly in place, then you will rejoice in what they have and be thankful for what you have as well.

Journal/Activity

Make a list of all your abilities, characteristics, friends, family, and possessions. Next to each of them, write why you are thankful for each. How can you develop the gifts you have rather than wishing you had the gifts of others?

Get the Facts First

My Life

Have you ever heard something said about someone else and assumed it was true? What did your assumptions lead you to do?

Setting the Scene

Matthew begins his Gospel with the origins of Jesus, starting with those who came before him and then the circumstances surrounding his birth.

Matthew 1:18-25

Reflection

You have to give Joseph credit. Even though he was acting out of ignorance, he still was concerned for Mary. He wished not to expose her to the law. According to the law, pregnancy would have meant her death. Sex outside of marriage was not tolerated in those days. Under the circumstances what else was Joseph to think? What would you have thought? Not too many of us would have assumed a miracle and neither did he. If it wasn't for the angel appearing, Joseph would have made a big mistake. When have you made a big mistake in a relationship because you didn't get all the facts straight?

Gossip has done more damage to relationships than anything else. When you hear something about someone for whom you care, don't assume it's true. Go directly to the person and find out the truth. Many times you'll find out that they have been misquoted or misunderstood. If they did say or do that which has upset you, then give them a chance to explain. You just don't know for sure unless you go to the source. If you find out the worst you may want to save your reaction. Give some thought to what this person means to you. The injury may not be as great as the relationship you have had.

Take It to God

Pray that you may not become part of the human grapevine. Pray that you would give your friends the benefit of the doubt. Pray for the courage to go to the source when you've heard a rumor and get the facts straight. Know that they, like you, are not perfect. Be willing to forgive if necessary.

Journal/Activity

Place yourself in Mary's situation. Record how you would have felt knowing the circumstances you are in, what people might think, and how Joseph stood by your side. Have you ever stood by a person's side in a difficult situation or had someone stand by you? How were you like Mary or Joseph in that situation?

Don't Drown Them with Your Feelings

My Life

Have you ever been bursting with feelings, in response to any given situation? Have you overwhelmed people with your emotions rather than being sensitive to how much they can handle?

Setting the Scene

We return to the story of Joseph and his brothers. On top of his father's affection, Joseph also enjoys a special relationship with God. Here we find Joseph overcome with excitement because God has spoken to him in a dream.

Genesis 37:5-8

Reflection

If you pour a month's supply of water on a plant you could drown it. In your enthusiasm, you may have given the plant all it needed for the month, but common sense would have told you that the plant couldn't handle all that water.

As we look further into Joseph's relationship with his family, he did the same thing. We already know of their jealousy, yet here he is telling them a dream in which he would be king over them. Now if Joseph was sensitive to their feelings, do you think he would have taken a different approach? Bursting on the scene with his emotions in this situation would be like hiring a comedian to do the eulogy at a funeral. It just isn't appropriate.

If you have a tendency to be emotional, moody, or temperamental, then you may be prone to over-react when your feelings are aroused. When you're upset, try the old custom of counting to ten before you react. If you feel hurt, give it some thought because it may not be as severe as your feelings are telling you. If you feel you need to communicate, guard your words. Don't drown the plant. Look at the situation and carefully decide which words accurately describe how you feel. You don't want to just speak, you want to be heard.

Take It to God

Pray that the sensitivity you have with regard to others' actions toward you may be channeled into sensitivity to their feelings as you respond to them. Pray that your feelings may not control you, but that you may control and use your feelings for good.

Journal/Activity

Think of the last time you were upset or excited and your words were taken the wrong way. Reconsider the situation and write down what you would say differently and how you would say it.

Help Each Other Along

My Life

Have you ever had a friend who was doing something that was hurting him or her or others? Did you find it difficult to approach them but you were concerned?

Setting the Scene

In this letter from Paul, the Galatians have just been told the difference between living in sin and living in God's love. Paul then talks to them about the attitude and approach we need to take toward those we love who are doing wrong.

Galatians 6:1-2

Reflection

These two short verses carry sensitivity, compassion, and love. You can almost sense here that Paul has been on both sides of this issue. He has been in sin and had someone blow him away with his self-righteous attitude. He may have tried to help someone in sin and fallen in the same trap himself. We're not just called to set each other straight. We're not called to share each other's sins. We are called to walk together and hold each other up. If this isn't friendship then what is?

How do you correct a friend in sin? The answer is in verse two. You don't approach the person for the purpose of correction. If your friend in Christ is faltering then there is probably something wrong. Are you concerned about the person? Ask what is troubling them. Be there as a friend. Be ready to listen and offer support. Spend some time together and pray for each other. Be willing to share yourself. Go as one who has burdens. Don't go as one who has it all together. No one has it all together but Jesus.

Take It to God

Together, reach out to Jesus who is our non-condemning friend. Seek his support. Pray today for a nonjudgmental attitude toward those in sin. Pray for sensitivity to the struggles of others. Pray for a sense of companionship toward your fellow Christians. Bear one another up and walk together in Christ.

Journal/Activity

Do you have a good friend that has been there with you when you have done something wrong? Write a letter to that friend thanking them and telling them what they mean to you. You could also call them up or go for a walk and tell them in person.

_____

_____

_____

_____

_____

_____

_____

_____

_____

_____

_____

_____

_____

_____

_____

_____

_____

_____

_____

_____

_____

The Degree of Our Love

My Life

Have you ever been in a situation when you were not the kind of friend you had hoped you would be; you really let a friend down?

Setting the Scene

We find ourselves in the middle of John's chapter recounting the final teachings of Jesus to his friends before he was taken away to die. Here we find Jesus sharing the things he wants them to remember before he leaves.

John 15:9-12

Reflection

A horse would not find its greatest joy in swimming. That's not what horses were made to do. A horse was made to run in an open field with the wind blowing through its mane. In the same way, an eagle would not find joy locked up in a cage. No, an eagle was made to soar high up in the sky, peering down on the earth. An eagle would be happy only if it could fly.

A person would not find joy in living for one's self. A person was not made for that. We were made to love each other. We were made to love unselfishly as Jesus himself loved us. If this was what we were made to do, then like the eagle who couldn't fly or the horse who couldn't run, we would not be happy if we did not love. No, we were made to love to the extent that we would give up our very selves for each other.

Examine the manner in which you love. Is it for the sake of others? Do you give expecting something in return? Do you put conditions on your giving? The manner in which Christ has loved us is a high calling. It is difficult for us to attain. The question is, Is it something we want? Jesus said that our joy would be complete in loving, and he used his loving as an example for us.

Take it to God

If we wish to be what we were created to be, we must love. Pray that God will increase both the desire and capacity to love within you that the degree of your love may grow towards that of Christ.

Journal/Activity

Imagine yourself spending a day with Jesus watching him interact with his friends and those he meets. Write an imaginary list of examples of how He shows love for others. How do you feel challenged by his example? Pray that He will help you to love others as He has loved you.

Learning to Forgive Is Important

My Life

Have you ever felt uncomfortable in a group of people because you got the impression that they thought they were better than you?

Setting the Scene

In this parable Jesus addresses the example of one person who sought understanding but did not realize his need to understand and have compassion for others.

Matthew 18:21-35

Reflection

This is the first parable I remember reading after my commitment to Christ. I had just returned from camp where I had a life-changing experience with Christ. Scripture meant so much to me and I was reading it daily. One day at work I was sharing about my experience and what Jesus meant to me when a girl whom everyone knew about asked me if I could ever date a girl who wasn't a virgin. Having just read this parable that day, I told her that since God has forgiven me all my sins how could I stand in judgment of someone else? You could see in her eyes such a feeling of relief at having been accepted and not judged, that God does forgive her. Often the forgiveness of Christ becomes known through our willingness to share his mercy.

How have you shown Christ to your friends through your willingness not to judge them?

Why do you feel you are better than them? Ask God to help you not to judge them for God has forgiven you your sins.

Take It to God

Pray that God may grant you a love for others that is rich enough to allow you to help your friends overcome their wrongdoing and not stand in judgment on them. Pray that God will forgive you your unwillingness to forgive. Pray that the wounds of past resentments in your friendships would be healed and a new attitude of acceptance would begin.

You're Worth It!

Journal/Activity

Write your own parable of forgiveness. Try and put it in a setting that relates to your life.

_____

_____

_____

_____

_____

_____

_____

_____

_____

_____

_____

_____

_____

_____

_____

_____

_____

_____

_____

_____

_____

_____

_____

_____

_____

_____

_____

_____

Adjusting to Changing Friends

My Life

It's not easy to adjust to shifting friendships. Have you and a friend ever drifted apart? Was it because either you or your friend changed and you resented how that change affected your friendship?

Setting the Scene

The Corinthians had the most conflict of any community to which Paul was writing. It is here that Paul wrote some of his best thoughts about how we should love one another.

1 Corinthians 13:11-13

Reflection

I just experienced reconciliation with a friend who has undergone a great deal of change lately. I had been critical of his change and we grew apart because of our differences. I eventually realized that we have both changed and it's not fair for either of us to judge the other.

We're all growing. We're children growing into spiritual adulthood. There will be more change in you between the ages of 13 and 22 than at any other time in your life. Your friends will change as well. If you grow in different directions, then maybe that's God's plan. You don't know what is going on in each other's hearts. It is for us to love in this time of change. If our focal point is Christ, we will grow from the experience.

Take It to God

Pray that you may be able to accept and love your friends as you both grow. Strive not to judge them, but to be a supporting friend whenever they need you. Pray for the companionship you need, especially when change has separated you from the companionship you had. Remain close to Christ, the friend who will never change.

Journal/Activity

Find a family album or box with your pictures as you are growing up. As you look through the different periods of your life, write down how you have changed until you come to the present. What gifts and abilities did you develop? How many friends did you make along the way? Without change there is no growth. Thank God for the changes in yourself and in others.

_____

_____

_____

_____

_____

_____

_____

_____

_____

_____

_____

_____

_____

_____

_____

_____

_____

_____

_____

Be Honest About Who You Are

My Life

Have you ever tried to be different than you really are because you wanted others to accept you?

Setting the Scene

We are early in Israel's history in this passage from 1 Samuel. David has not yet become king. He is just a shepherd boy. Because of his great love for God and God's people, David has answered the call to fight Goliath.

1 Samuel 17:38-40

Reflection

David must have looked quite comical in Saul's armor. The armor didn't fit. Trying to go out and fight like Saul just wasn't going to work for David. He finally stripped himself of Saul's gear and picked up five small stones. He would fight Goliath, the giant, as a shepherd boy for that was who he was.

How often do we try to be someone we are not? We arm ourselves with their characteristics thinking that we'll be more successful if we do. We see someone with a great sense of humor. Their acceptance is great. They make people laugh. We wish we could be as popular as they are.

If we try to be funny and we are not, we'll bomb. If we try and be someone we are not and get accepted, it's only temporary. People will get to know us as we really are. If they accepted the false image, then the real thing might not be appreciated.

David was a shepherd boy, but that was good enough. He knew he couldn't pretend to be someone he wasn't. We know the story, so we know the success. He defeated the giant.

Accept who you are. If you don't, no one else will. God made you and as meager as that may seem to you, it's still a lot. Be honest about who you are with others. In the end, those who accept you will accept you for who you are. Those friendships will mean much more and you'll be happier in the end.

Take It to God

Pray that God may enable you not to wear a mask, but to be yourself with the people you meet.

Journal/Activity

Draw a picture(s) or describe the different masks that you wear. Do each one on a separate sheet of paper. As you go through the next few days, be honest about how you feel and who you are around others. Be gentle, you might catch someone by surprise. As you unveil the true you, throw away the picture or the description of the masks until they're all gone.

_____

_____

_____

_____

_____

_____

_____

_____

_____

_____

_____

_____

_____

_____

Saying Good-Bye

My Life

Have you ever said goodbye to a good friend?

Setting the Scene

Before David became king he developed a very close friendship with King Saul's son, Jonathan. Saul's jealousy of David placed David in danger and drove David and Jonathan apart.

1 Samuel 20:38-42

Reflection

After my senior year in high school, I worked at a camp for one month. I made many friends, but one in particular meant the most. He worked on the pit crew with me. He washed dishes. Saying good-bye wasn't easy, but we knew it wouldn't be permanent. We wrote each other almost every other week. After a couple of years he came to visit me. We had a great time and saying good-bye was tough again. I wrote a few more times but there was no reply. I saw a mutual friend a few years later, but he knew nothing about where he was. I still don't know what happened. I do miss him. We built quite a friendship over those years. We shared a lot. But life went on and I made many new friends.

David and Jonathan were saying good-bye. It wasn't forever, but when you part sometimes you think it will be. It was hard, but they did it. If you read through the rest of Samuel, you will see that their friendship ended up being of great value. Their lives went on and they grew in their friendship.

You will have to say good-bye to friends. You may have already done that. It is not easy, but like David and Jonathan, you will go on. Along with the sorrow you feel over the departure, be thankful for the friendship you have had. Know that through knowing and sharing each other you are a better person.

Take It to God

Pray that God will bless your friend as you go on and pray that what you learned in your relationship will enhance the relationships you'll have in the future.

Journal/Activity

Write a letter to a friend to whom you have said good-bye. Don't forget to mail it.

God Is with You

My Life

Think back and recall the people that you have been closest to in your life. How have they affected the way you feel and act?

Setting the Scene

At the end of Matthew's Gospel, Jesus is saying good-bye to the friends he has been closest to during his life.

Matthew 28:20

Reflection

We are an accumulation of the experiences we have had. Most of those experiences revolve around people we've known. Their influence has helped to form our values and our personality. They leave a deep impression even after they are gone. Parents would rank high on that list of influential people in our lives. Teachers and others in positions of authority would be on that list. And of course close friends.

The Apostles here are seeing Jesus for the last time. Without question He had to be the most influential friend in their lives. For three years they ate, slept, and walked the countryside with Him, living a new way of life. What they became was shaped in large part by Jesus. The most important thing He gave his Apostles is something that no one but Jesus could give. He promised His presence until the end of time.

The Holy Spirit is God with us. Unlike our friends, His presence is always with us, always helping us grow.

Take It to God

As you reflect on the influence that others have had on you, thank God for the time you've known them. For those still present in your life, know that they won't always be there, so learn all you can from those relationships. Above all, pray that the presence of God with you may always be your primary source of formation. Take comfort in His presence, for He will never leave you.

Journal/Activity

Take a walk and note in creation all the signs of God's presence around you. Afterward go sit in a quiet space and think about the God who created all that there is.

You're Worth It!

Chapter V
Dating Relationships

The LORD God said: It is not good for the man to be alone.
I will make a helper suited to him. (Gn 2:18)

Have Something in Common

My Life

What is the first thing that you pay attention to when you see a member of the opposite sex?

Setting the Scene

Back to the Corinthian community. Paul had to speak to the Corinthians often regarding relationship problems.

2 Corinthians 6:14-18

Reflection

Now let's be honest, sometimes we see someone to whom we are instantly attracted. Nothing wrong with that. The problem arises when the beauty of the flesh is the criteria for dating relationships. If the basis of choosing dates is only skin-deep, then the basis of the relationships will be shallow as well. If we want our dating relationships to be more substantial, then the two people must have something in common.

Having something in common will make dating both enjoyable and meaningful. The more you have in common, the more easily you will share with each other. Dating relationships develop more easily among those who have known each other and are drawn together by their common interests and personalities. Physical attraction is certainly a part of a dating relationship, but it cannot sustain it.

For a Christian, there is nothing more important than Jesus and your relationship with him. In a dating relationship, when you share so much of yourself, if you don't have Christian values and a relationship with Jesus in common, there is a limit to the depth of the relationship. Either the Christian will have to compromise or give in to the non-Christian values in order to maintain the relationship. If there is no strain within the relationship, or if the non-believer doesn't change and believe, then it is time for you to examine whether you have compromised on your relationship with God.

You're Worth It!

Take It to God

Pray that God may help you to see the importance of Christian dating and its effect on the quality of your relationships. Allow common interests, especially your faith, to be the foundation of your relationships. Learn to be friends first, and allow God to guide your relationship.

Journal/Activity

Write down three members of the opposite sex with whom you feel the most at ease in being yourself. Time flies and it's enjoyable to be with them. Write down what you have in common with each. Listen and find out what they value and what they believe.

How Much Has Really Changed?

My Life

Do you find it difficult to maintain your commitment to living a Christian life when so many people you know disagree? Do you begin to question whether you are right?

Setting the Scene

The community that John writes to in this passage is one that claims to be Christian but does not agree with the life of the Gospel. John writes to them about the basic beliefs of our faith and how they should influence the way we live our lives.

1 John 2:15-17

Reflection

Surprise! Two thousand years ago they were saying the same things and having the same problems we have today. In the time of Christ, the morality of society was opposed to him. Today, what many call a new morality isn't new at all. It consists of the same values that Christ condemned back then.

Immorality seems to flourish today. We can't deny that. We've become more open about it, and many temptations are all around us. Along with the rejection of Christian values has come the breakdown of families and extended families. We no longer value human life whether we're liberal or conservative. One promotes abortion and the other the death penalty. We don't want to listen to God's Word but God has good reason for the guidelines he has given us.

Sex has its purpose and it's not entertainment. We need only look around us to see the results of a society without values. Teenagers are not proud after an abortion. Deep inside, a loose reputation doesn't feel good. As long as we go the way of the world we won't be happy and we won't find peace with God.

Take It to God

God calls us to place our lives with him and reject the immorality of society. Pray that God will strengthen your integrity. Pray that you

You're Worth It!

will be able to look beyond the immediate pleasures for a joy that lasts forever. Allow your dating relationships to be built on Christ and the values you share in common with him.

Journal/Activity

Rent the movie "Man of La Mancha." Note how the hero struggled against all odds to remain faithful to what he believed. Let the movie inspire you to do the same.

_____

_____

_____

_____

_____

_____

_____

_____

_____

_____

_____

_____

_____

_____

_____

_____

_____

_____

_____

Sex Was God's Idea

My Life

Do you sometimes listen to other Christians talk about sex and get the idea that there is something wrong with it?

Setting the Scene

Here in Genesis we find the stories of the origin of humanity. Along with it we find the belief that what God created was good and it included his will for men and women together.

Genesis 2:18

Reflection

To hear some Christians talk about sex you would think it's a sin. I have good news. Sex was God's idea. Let's hear three cheers for God! He could have made us like fish. Mama fish swims through the water, stops, drops off some eggs, and swims away. Papa fish swims along, ejects his sperm into the eggs, and off he goes. Not exactly material for restricted audiences is it? When God made us, he obviously had something else in mind. He wanted it to be pleasurable. I'm not saying that sexual activity can't be sinful. Anything involving a human act contains the potential for good or evil. Sexual activity is sinful when it doesn't fulfill the purpose for which God created it. The purpose for which God created sex is twofold. One, it must be an act of committed love. Two, it must be life giving and from this ongoing relationship of life-giving love comes human life. If you have not the desire for children and the love for which this union is intended then your sexual union is not what God desires.

Take It to God

Do you feel like I took the good news away? Don't feel bad. I couldn't just tell you sex was God's idea unless I told you what the idea was. For today, take time to thank God for sex, and the fact that he made it pleasurable, a union of love. Pray that God will enable you to save the act of love for the person you will love forever.

You're Worth It!

Journal/Activity

Write down three examples of life situations that are affected by the absence of love. Write down three examples of how love enriches a life situation. Now reflect on the wisdom of God making the ultimate expression of love life-giving.

Enjoy it within Commitment

My Life

Think about the commitment necessary to be involved with a team, a band, a choir, a musical, or a job Can you remain a part of these activities without the commitment it takes?

Setting the Scene

We find ourselves back with the stories of human origin and the origin of the relationship between man and woman.

Genesis 2:21-24

Reflection

One life is drawn from another and in their coming together they are one again. A giving of one's self that is so complete that they are no longer seen as two but one flesh. The marriage of husband and wife is a total union of their lives, consummated and signed in their sexual union. Within this commitment can love be understood, a total giving of one to another.

In conversations concerning premarital sex I have often stated that sexual intercourse should only be experienced between husband and wife. People living together outside of marriage object to this view and say that they love each other. I respond that they should get married to which they say that they can't make a commitment. If you can't make a commitment, then is your love sufficient for one another? Love is giving one to another with no strings attached. Sexual love is a total giving of one self to another person without withdrawing that gift. Do you belong to each other? That's what marriage is. Outside of that commitment the meaning of sexual intercourse is diminished. God made sex to be experienced within commitment, total self-giving love.

Take It to God

Pray that the sexual desires you have within you and within your dating relationships may not cause you to cheapen the gift you will offer to the person you will love forever. Begin to love that person

You're Worth It!

whom you will someday marry now. Even if you have already given in to sexual relationships, begin now to save yourself for your future spouse. Pray to God for a renewed commitment to him. With God and his merciful love we can always start over.

Journal/Activity

Write a letter to your future spouse even if you don't know that person now. Promise that person, that out of your commitment of love you promise to save yourself until your wedding night.

Keep It Natural

My Life

Have you ever been in a situation that you wish you weren't in because of what could happen?

Setting the Scene

In his most famous sermon, the Sermon on the Mount, Jesus goes through a series of situations in which he compares what the law requires and then states what he adds in addition. In these sayings Jesus examines the root of our actions.

Matthew 5:27-30

Reflection

If you fast for three days and then sit down to eat, you won't be able to eat as much as you'd think. Because of not eating for so long, your stomach has shrunk. After eating for a few days, you'll stretch it back out and have your normal appetite again. Your sexual appetite isn't much different. Building up a sexual appetite can create a desire which feels a need to be met. Jesus addresses this problem in his sermon. Lusting after the woman is the beginning of the sin. The actions that follow are a natural response to an overfed desire.

The building of the desire isn't necessary. God has created us all with a natural built-in desire which begins when puberty starts and continues to grow into our adult life. If God created it, then a natural level of sexual desire is a gift from God and is good. The fulfillment of that desire is rightfully completed in the unselfish act of married love. The selfish completion of that desire, then, is sin. If that is true, then so is any act that makes it more difficult to wait until we are married.

Masturbation is the most common means of building an unnatural sex drive. Someone who masturbates daily won't be satisfied with holding hands for long. Foreplay is in much the same category except it involves another person. Heavy kissing and petting build a desire which leads to sexual intercourse. That's why it's called foreplay. Even if the person doesn't go on to intercourse, he or she has already used their sexual power to complete their own desires.

Before going on a guilt trip, know that it isn't easy. Most teenagers have masturbated. That doesn't make it right. The natural desire is hard to control at times and God understands. What you must do is make every effort possible to control your desire for the sake of the values you hold and the person you are forming — you. Pornography, then, is out. If you strive to be pure then don't build unnatural desires.

Take It to God

If you falter, God will help you if you turn to him for help. Pray that God will enable you to resist those things and activities which accelerate your sex drive. Learn to be pure in heart yet thankful for the sexual appetite which God has given you.

Journal/Activity

Throw out anything you have in your life that accelerates your sexual appetite. That includes posters, magazines with sensual pictures, videos, stories, or articles. In other words, get rid of the sexual junk food in your life.

_____

_____

_____

_____

_____

_____

_____

_____

_____

_____

_____

It's Worth Waiting For

My Life

When you were a little kid and eating a lot of junk food, did your Mom say you were going to spoil your dinner? Of course, when you're having liver and onions what's to spoil?

Setting the Scene

In the next few chapters of the letter to the Romans we find Paul giving guidance on overcoming evil in our lives, the struggle it entails, and the strength and guidance we have from God. Rome was a community that Paul had not visited, and in his letter to them he expounds on many of the basic teachings of the Christian faith.

Romans 6:12

Reflection

I'm half Syrian and I love Syrian food. When Mom made rolled grape leaves for dinner no one had to yell at me about eating junk food. I'd skip lunch so I could eat more grape leaves at dinner.

There aren't too many things for which we'll put off instant satisfaction. Fast food restaurants, television, and movies satisfy us all too quickly. When we take our experience of instant gratification into our personal life, we find the same desires there. Being used to getting what we want now, the temptation is even stronger. For what in your life are you willing to sacrifice? In sports you learn to sacrifice so that you may win. In school you learn to sacrifice now for a possible career. In relation to sex, what is the motivation for putting off intercourse? What is our goal?

Being chaste and waiting until marriage was important to me. I wanted to be able to give myself to my wife, knowing that she was the only one. I wanted that moment to be uniquely special. No one else could ever share that moment. I knew someday I would love somebody more than anyone else and I was right. Believe me, putting off sex until my wedding night held a much higher reward than skipping lunch for the rolled grape leaves.

Take It to God

Instant gratification often lessens the value of a later experience. Pray that God may give you a vision of what can be. Learn to sacrifice now for what you will have later. Let your hopes and desires culminate with the one you will love more than any other.

Journal/Activity

Take a walk down memory lane to an early childhood Christmas. Picture the wait until Christmas morning. Remember the excitement of opening the gifts and how it made you feel. You have another gift to open on your wedding night. Don't open it early.

_____

_____

_____

_____

_____

_____

_____

_____

_____

_____

_____

_____

_____

_____

_____

_____

What If I Didn't Wait?

My Life

Have you ever done anything that made you feel so bad that you were overwhelmed with guilt? Did you find it difficult to talk to God?

Setting the Scene

The story of the woman caught in adultery is a famous story of God's compassion for us and Jesus' rejection of the condemnation we bring on ourselves and others.

John 8:3-11

Reflection

We Christians condemn those guilty of sexual sins so much more quickly than any other. Maybe it's out of fear. The temptation to sin is so strong, because of our sex drives, that we make it the worst of evils in order to scare off potential actions. Because of that drive, the sin may be less serious, but the consequences on our lives can still be very serious. No matter what, we have to remember how much God loves us and forgives all our sins.

In this passage, Jesus is presented with an adulterous woman. The scribes brought her for the sake of condemnation. Many theologians believe that when Jesus was writing on the ground he was writing the sins of the Pharisees. One by one they left, leaving Jesus alone with her. Jesus did not condemn her but accepted her as she was, telling her to sin no more. He did not compromise on the truth. What she did was wrong, but there was a greater truth. He loved her.

Jesus accepts you where you are at, even if you have fallen. Turn to Jesus. He will never condemn you, but only greet you with love and forgiveness. You may need healing within. Allow Jesus to touch your heart and mind to help you feel whole. You can go on from here and begin anew. Begin today to save yourself for the one you'll love forever and know that your wedding night will be beautiful.

Take It to God

Pray that God may help you to see how good you are. Open your heart to Him and let His Spirit fill you. Know that you belong to God. Know that you are a new creation with a new beginning. Pray for healing and accept the forgiveness that God rushes to give you.

Journal/Activity

Sometimes we perceive a lack of forgiveness from God because we do not forgive ourselves. Write a letter of forgiveness to yourself. Whenever you feel any guilt for past sins read it to yourself. Forgiveness is the key to freedom from sin.

The Right Way to Break Up

My Life

How many times have you seen a couple that you couldn't pry apart with a crowbar break up and then rip apart each other's reputations? They were the class couple. Now they are the *Terminator* against the *Predator*. What happened to them? Why can't they just stop dating and be friends? More often than not, they probably weren't friends to begin with.

Setting the Scene

The story of Samson and Delilah is a story about an impulsive desire and commitment that led to the destruction of a person's life. Here in these verses you have the beginning of the destructive relationship of Samson and Delilah.

Judges 16:4-5

Reflection

Overcommitment, at too early an age or too early in a dating relationship, is a big mistake. Sometimes a couple decides to exclusively date but no real relationship has developed. There's no foundation, no friendship on which to base their time together. Physical attraction and a decent personality serve as cornerstones. When they break up, there's nothing to fall back on.

Learn to develop friendships with members of the opposite sex. Go out and have a good time. Get to know each other. Let the depth of the relationship grow naturally. Trust is based on experiencing the other person and finding them trustworthy. Only then should you open up to that person. It takes time. Out of all your friends of the opposite sex, those with whom you have the most in common and share the deepest friendships will become those you date. When that type of friendship is the foundation of your dating relationship, you stand a better chance of being friends when you break up.

Take It to God

Pray that God would grant you a kind heart at times when relationships are strained. Pray that when you break up you can learn to see the good in that person and remain their friend. Learn not to over-commit too soon. The key to breaking up is to start out right in the first place.

Journal/Activity

Write down ten characteristics you want in a friend. When you are attracted to a member of the opposite sex, check to see if that person has the characteristics on your list.

A New Day

My Life

Have you ever found it difficult to let go of something because it is what you are used to? Even if you know it's not good for you, it is hard to change.

Setting the Scene

The story of Sodom and Gomorrah culminates with the destruction of the evil towns and Lot's family escaping to a nearby town for safety. For a time Sodom had become their home. Although they knew that they needed to flee for safety, it was still difficult to let go.

Genesis 19:20-26

Reflection

Don't let yesterday's mistakes haunt today's new beginnings. Don't dwell on the past. It's gone. You can't change yesterday, so don't relive it. Lot's wife looked back and became a pillar of salt. She could not go on and neither will we be able to grow if we don't live in the moment of today. Seek to be a new person within the relationships of your life. Hold on to what is good and relinquish those mistakes that hurt you.

In relation to your parents, learn to listen and to share. Keep your emotions in check. When difficulties come, it's nice to have a stable relationship with a parent to fall back on.

With your friends, take off your mask and be yourself. The friends you will have will be those who accept you for who you are. Life is so much easier when you have friends who don't pressure you to conform, but let the unique qualities you have come through.

Learn to have friends of the opposite sex. Be up front from the start and you'll be drawn to those who will really care about who you are. Don't commit too soon. Let the relationships develop on their own.

Take It to God

Pray that you may be able to love your parents when they seem to be most demanding. Pray that their relationship with one another may be strong. Help to keep God in the center of your home.

You're Worth It!

Pray that you can share Christ with your closest friends and that those friendships will draw you closer to God.

Pray that God may draw you together with partners who share your faith. Share that faith together. Take time to thank God for the friends and family you have. Thank him for each individual person, one at a time, and also pray for their needs. Commit your relationships to God that he may draw you closer to him.

Journal/Activity

Make a list of your friends, family and other important people in your life. Write down one quality in each of them that you admire. Thank God for how they have touched your life.

You're Worth It!

Chapter VI
Fellowship in God's Family

He will wipe every tear from their eyes, and there shall be no more death or mourning, wailing or pain, [for] the old order has passed away. (Rev. 21:4)

I Know You

My Life

Have you ever had a friendship so special that even if you are apart for a long time, when you see each other again it's like you have never been apart?

Setting the Scene

In this passage from Matthew Jesus is told that his family is outside waiting for him. He has been among the people sharing the Good News of God's Kingdom.

Matthew 12:46-50

Reflection

I Know You

I know you.
I know your heart too well.
A common thread runs between us.
Spun form the same spinning wheel.
Our form varies
but from the same hand we came.
Outward appearance deceives not,
inward we are one.
We depart.
Our communion is at an end.
Yet will I always know you,
My brother, my sister, my friend.

Within all Christians is the same common, trait of friendship with Jesus. Because of that common bond, we are family. We share values, beliefs, and priorities. We have similar goals. We are different, but within us is a sense of belonging to God and one another.

The Church is God's family. If you belong to God, you belong to the family. Get to know your other family. Draw from it the friendships you need to be close to God.

Take It to God

Pray that God may lead you into fellowship with your brothers and sisters in Christ. Being with peers, who share Christ in common, will enable you to feel a stronger sense of awareness of God in your daily life.

Journal/Activity

What are the common goals that draw a team together and unify them? What are the common goals of Christians? Using the example of a team, what do Christians need to do to reach their common goals?

_____

_____

_____

_____

_____

_____

_____

_____

_____

_____

_____

_____

_____

_____

_____

_____

_____

_____

_____

How Does It Help Me?

My Life

Do you find that you act differently around different people?

Setting the Scene

In Chapter 15 of John's Gospel Jesus begins his teaching on a disciples love with the story of the vine and the branches.

John 15:1-15

Reflection

I saw an illustration that depicts an internal battle of good and evil within us. Within us there are two dogs that are constantly fighting. Do you wonder which one will win? The one you feed the most. Simple as that sounds, it makes an issue that we tend to complicate more readily understood. In our struggle between following Christ and not following him, we need to nourish our tendency to follow him more than our tendency not to. If we do, Christ within us will win.

The influences that cause us not to be Christian are many. Much of our music, films, and other forms of entertainment promote a valueless society. Peer pressure to conform robs us of our individuality. The stress of conflicts in relationships causes us to seek escapes from reality in the form of drugs and alcohol. This tide must be stemmed. We need the support of peers who seek the same lifestyle so we know we're not alone.

It is a relief to be able to spend time in a group of people where Christian values are the norm. It is an added bonus to be able to share our struggles with each other in order to gain understanding and help. A solid peer support group within our church can be just what we need.

According to John 15, in being part of the vine, we are pruned that we may bear fruit. Our problems and our faults can be shared and prayed for. Dealing with conflict within a Christian group can help to expose our faults in an atmosphere where we can deal with them. Learning to love your neighbor within close community isn't always easy, but the reward is worth it. Within us the right dog will win.

Take It to God

Pray for a support group for teens to form in your church. Gather together with other teens in your parish and seek who will work with you. Keep knocking on the pastor's door until he doesn't have a choice. With the help of adults who will work with you, one of the greatest tools of Christian growth can be yours — each other.

Journal/Activity

Make a list of potential adults and teens with whom you can form a peer support group in your church. If there is one already, join it. If there are others like you with the same need, then invite them along.

_____

_____

_____

_____

_____

_____

_____

_____

_____

_____

_____

_____

_____

_____

_____

_____

The Good In Each of Us

My Life

Have you ever met someone you heard was a terrible person and so you thought he was? Once you met that person, you discovered he was a nice person just misunderstood?

Setting the Scene

As Jesus traveled and preached, he touched the lives of many people. In this story, he touches the life of Zacchaeus the tax collector. Tax collectors in Jesus' time were viewed as traitors to their people because they collected taxes for the Romans.

Luke 19:1-10

I once heard an analogy of the Church on a taped talk from Archbishop Fulton Sheen. He compared the Church to a hospital. You can go into a hospital and see suffering, pain, illness and death. Or you can go into the same hospital and see kindness, healing and life. We can do the same with a parish community or an individual. We can look for faults and place blame. We can judge, condemn and think the worst of others. Or we can see the good in people, the growth, the potential and be appreciative of the goodness there.

Zacchaeus was a tax collector. Nobody could have a worse reputation, yet Jesus saw good in him. He came to have supper with him and announced salvation was his. While Jesus was bringing Zacchaeus hope, the towns people were condemning him. We do the same with each other when we're quick to judge. Jesus, as with Zacchaeus, sees the good in each of us and gives us reason to have hope.

Take it to God

Pray that your attitude towards your church group will be positive. Recognize that the faults in your community are shared by you as well. Know this also can be a sign, as with Christ and Zacchaeus, that sinners are welcome. It is here they find hope, and it is here that we can all grow together.

Journal/Activity

Think of the most positive person you know and the most negative person you know. Who is the happiest? Decide which one you want to emulate.

_____

_____

_____

_____

_____

_____

_____

_____

_____

_____

_____

_____

_____

_____

_____

_____

_____

_____

_____

_____

_____

_____

_____

They Know How I Feel

My Life

Have you ever been traveling on vacation quite far from home and run across someone from your home state? You've never met before, but there is still an instant attraction. Perhaps you will stop and talk for a few minutes. You may still be strangers, but because you come from the same place, you feel a sense of camaraderie.

Setting the Scene

This is the second Christian community described in the Book of Acts. In each case the preaching and acceptance of the Gospel was followed by the formation of Christian community.

Acts 4:32-35

Reflection

A sense of camaraderie is more evident within Christian community. Within a youth group, there is much you have in common. You share much of the same beliefs. Values are similar and you see God as the central focus of your life. If you saw someone from your group in an unexpected place, the sense of joyful surprise would indicate that unity. As verse 32 in this reading says, you begin to become one in heart and mind.

The oneness leads to a sense of understanding as you go through the same struggles together. Prayer together means more. You can sense the sincerity. As people seek to understand each other, you can sense that they are accomplishing that goal. You begin to hold one another up and meet each other's needs.

Take It to God

Pray that as your group grows closer together, you may be more of one mind and heart. Allow concern for one another to grow. Learn to listen to each other's needs. Because you share so many of the same problems and also share the same solution, Jesus Christ, you'll find a unity of friendship that couldn't be better.

Journal/Activity

Prayer helps build community. Make a prayer list of the members of a group you are in. At least once a week pray for the members of your group and any particular needs that you may be aware of.

Thanks God, I Needed That!

My Life

Have you ever stopped and dreamt what heaven must be like?

Setting the Scene

The Book of Revelation is a symbolic writing to the early Christians who were suffering great persecution. They needed words of hope to continue through the struggles of their lives. Part of their hope rested in dreaming of what awaits them at the end of their struggle, of what heaven must be like.

Revelation 21:1-7

Reflection

In verse 4, God brings us comfort and hope. The wiping of the tear from our eyes and the promise of no more pain holds for the end of time, but his consolation is also present in the midst of all our trials. The imagery continues in verses 6-7 where God promises to quench our thirst and give us our inheritance, life with him. This is all an image of the place he spoke of in John 14. What sense of heaven do you get from Revelation? What will be no more? For what do you thirst? How then will God quench your thirst? How has He in the past?

Every time we experience God, we get a taste of heaven. Every time He makes us feel whole and clean, we get a taste of that thirst-quenching water. Every time we leave behind old sins that gave us pain, we begin to sense what it will be like to have no more pain. The joy of heaven is not pie in the sky. It begins now and finds its fulfillment in heaven.

The last image to reflect on is in verse 2. The new city, which is symbolic of the church, God's people, is prepared as a bride. Jesus, in other passages of Scripture, is the bridegroom. In order to portray the love relationship between God and us, God uses the image of a bride and bridegroom preparing for marriage. Can you sense in these seven verses the ultimate sign of God's love for us? Can you sense His commitment to you?

You're Worth It!

Take It to God

Bring your pain, your sins, and all your sorrows to Christ. He will make you all new. He will prepare you for a forever filled with love. He will also help you to have a lifetime filled with love. Whenever you go through any trial, know that some of your heaven can come to earth. Pray for a union with Christ. Allow Him to wipe every tear from your eye. Learn to walk with him as part of that New Jerusalem, your brothers and sisters in Christ.

Journal/Activity

Go for a walk with Jesus today. During your time alone with Him know that He is walking with you. Share whatever sorrows you have and let his presence be a comfort. Know that through your time alone with him and with your church, Christ will always be with you.

_____

_____

_____

_____

_____

_____

_____

_____

_____

_____

_____

_____

_____

You're Worth It!

Chapter VII
Christian Discipleship

What good is it, my brothers, if someone says he has faith but does not have works? Can that faith save him? If a brother or sister has nothing to wear and has no food for the day, and one of you says to them, "Go in peace, keep warm, and eat well," but you do not give them the necessities of the body, what good is it? So also faith of itself, if it does not have works, is dead. (Jas 2:14-17)

Don't Just Say It

My Life

Think of someone you really trust. Do you trust them because of what they say or because of what they do?

Setting the Scene

In this letter of James, one of the main subjects is Christians who do not live the Christian faith yet claim to believe. That theme is directly addressed in this chapter.

James 2:14-17

Reflection

If you really believed in a friend you would stand by him, even if no one else did. If he was accused of cheating on a test at school and continuously denied doing it, you'd believe him even if you were the only one. When you know someone well and you know you can trust them, you believe in them no matter how bad it looks. Do you believe in Christ?

I've met so many people who say they believe in God yet they don't even know him. Without knowing His Word and spending time with Jesus in prayer, how can we believe in him? Without acting on His Word, who's going to believe we are the Christians we say we are? In James the meaning of a true life-giving faith is revealed. Christianity is not a religion of mere words, but one of faith in action, signs of God's love.

I can't just pray for the poor, but I must help the poor in any way I can. I can't just pray for my friends when they're in trouble, but I must stand by them. I can't just pray for broken relationships, but I must be present where I can be a means of reconciliation.

Take It to God

For whom have you prayed? What can you do to help your prayer take action? You are God's instrument for answering prayer more than you might think. Each time you pray for someone ask God to show what you can do to make the answer to that prayer a reality.

When you are certain of what God would have you do, act on it prayerfully, with faith.

Journal/Activity

Pick one thing you thought of that you can do and do it. Look at a calendar and figure out when you can act on your faith and call who you need to call to make it happen. Start with something that is simple and build from there.

_____

_____

_____

_____

_____

_____

_____

_____

_____

_____

_____

_____

_____

_____

_____

_____

_____

_____

The Blessings Will Come

My Life

When you look back on your life will you know in your heart that you lived for others? Did you put God first? Did you love Him? Did you love others? Will the answer to those questions be "yes"?

Setting the Scene

The Beatitudes are the core of the Sermon on the Mount. For many they stand as the foundation of Christian living and it is here that Jesus' most famous sermon begins.

Matthew 5:3-12

Reflection

Jesus addresses our heart in the Beatitudes. He claims that our joy lies in seeking Him and helping others. Do you seek to bring peace between your friends? Do you seek to heal hurts within your home? Are you willing to be hurt for the sake of loving? If your answer is "yes," then you will be happy and you will be blessed.

Take It to God

The Beatitudes are the essence of the Christian life and the sharing of ourselves with others. Read through each Beatitude and pray that God may help you to apply each to your life. Hunger and thirst for God. Seek to share with others. Pray that God's Spirit will be with you as you live a life of loving. Pray that as your life on earth ends, you will be at peace knowing you lived for God and others.

Journal/Activity

Write a practical example from your life of how you can live out each of the Beatitudes. Pick one that you can work on that won't add anything to your schedule. Circle it and check back in a week to see how you are doing.

You're Worth It!

You're Really Needed

My Life

Do you know others who seem lost and don't know where to find help when they need it?

Setting the Scene

We find here in Matthew's Gospel a moment of reflection for Jesus. He has preached, healed, and brought freedom to many but there are so many more. He needs others to reach out to them and so he sends out his disciples.

Matthew 9:35-38

Reflection

Is it so hard to see the harvest? Look around your school. Are there people with problems who don't know where to turn? They might turn to booze and parties. Sure they think they escape by getting drunk. They could wind up facing the same problems and more. Are there people who have lost friends? They need someone to be there to assure them of other friendships. Have your friends got problems that they can't handle by themselves? That is the harvest. They need someone. They need love now. How long can someone hide in a bottle? How long can people deal with problems without a solution? Jesus saw this in the villages and towns he visited. People were hurt, lonely, and exhausted by the weight of their problems. Jesus knew that he and the Apostles were not enough. He asked them to pray for more disciples. Will you be an answer to their prayer?

You and I are the instruments through which God speaks and heals others. You don't have to look to the poor in other countries. It is good to do what you can for them, but don't neglect the harvest in your own neighborhood. Answer God's call. Become more than just a person who has been forgiven and touched by God. Do more than share the good things that have happened to you. Reach out and touch those near you. You are needed. This isn't something extra in the Christian faith, but it is its fulfillment.

You're Worth It!

Take It to God

Pray that God may show you those who are hurting and need love. Pray for the compassion to reach out to pray for a filling of God's Spirit, enabling you to be his disciple.

Journal/Activity

The spiritual and corporal works of mercy have given Christians a summary of how they can show compassion for others. Ask your teacher or pastor for a list of them and see what works of mercy apply to your everyday life right now.

My Brother's Keeper

My Life

It's one thing to say nice things to people, but when someone you care for is hurting themselves by doing something you know is wrong, it's a lot tougher. Do you find at those times that the fear of losing a friendship often prevails and you don't say anything?

Setting the Scene

We see here in the call of the prophet Ezekiel a challenge that stands not only at the core of being a prophet but a lesson about being a true friend.

Ezekiel 3:17-21

Reflection

One of the most common mistakes I see friends doing today is drinking. How many friends do you have who go out to drinking parties during the week and on the weekends? Worse yet, sometimes they drink and drive, risking their life and others. How do you tell them that they are doing something wrong?

One of the first things you can do is put their well-being ahead of the friendship they offer you. If you really love them then you must act on their behalf. What good is your friendship if it will allow them to ruin their lives without speaking? There is a risk but aren't they worth it?

Second, be sensitive and act out of love. Don't condemn them, but only what they are doing. Recognize that they may have a problem or need and they are wrongly choosing to deal with it by drinking. Hurting and condemning remarks may only serve as an excuse for them to drink again.

There are other things about which you must speak out as well. Assure them of your friendship and love. Express your concern about what they are doing to themselves. Offer your help with whatever is troubling them. In all cases, speak out against the action and not the person. People need love and correction, not condemnation.

Take It to God

Pray that God may give you sensitive words to speak in delicate situations.

Journal/Activity

If you have a friend with a serious problem, talk to a school counselor or church leader about what is available for help. They may be able to help you help a friend.

Learning to Serve

My Life

Think of something that you enjoy doing but want to improve at. Who would you ask to help you improve?

Setting the Scene

According to John's Gospel, Jesus begins the Last Supper with washing his Apostles' feet, a symbolic ritual of hospitality and service.

John 13:3-15

Reflection

If I wanted to learn how to hit a baseball, I'd see Ken Griffey Jr., and Monica Seles could show me a few things about tennis. I wouldn't have any trouble listening to these people simply because they're such great examples of what I would want to learn. You can respect those who teach what they have mastered.

Jesus mastered the art of serving and loving others. In this passage of washing the disciples' feet, he explains this quite simply. It is by his example that he teaches. We are to teach others as well. We are to show what friendship is to our friends and what justice is to the unjust. If we are not loving to those we teach to love, what credibility do we have as a teacher? The best way to teach is by example.

What is it that you want to show others? Do you want your friends to learn to listen? You must listen to them. Do you want others to be treated with kindness? You must be kind to them.

Take It to God

Pray that God would teach you to have an attitude of service toward others so that by your example others may learn to serve. When you experience a lack of Christian virtue in another person, pray that you may be strong in that virtue as an example to them.

Journal/Activity

Imagine yourself as one of the Apostles and Jesus begins to wash

You're Worth It!

your feet. How would you respond? Write how this passage may have been different if you were there.

_____

_____

_____

_____

_____

_____

_____

_____

_____

_____

_____

_____

_____

_____

_____

_____

_____

_____

_____

_____

You Can Make a Difference

My Life

Have you ever been around someone who has to do everything by himself or herself? How does that affect those around him/her?

Setting the Scene

Moses was called by God to lead his people out of bondage. The next step was learning to become a people who were no longer slaves. They needed to learn to be on their own and had much to learn.

Exodus 18:13-22

Reflection

Moses was guilty of the messiah complex as much as anyone. It's great that he was concerned about the needs of others. It is also great that he wanted to convey God's Word. But in trying to do it all himself, he prevented other God-fearing people from being used by God. He also laid a great burden on the people and wore himself out trying to help them. His father-in-law gave him good advice.

By learning to delegate the work and learning to cooperate with others, Moses was left to address the most urgent needs. Other needs were met far more quickly because of the new help provided and many more talents and gifts were discovered in others who never had the chance to use them.

Do you try and play savior? Are you going to solve all the problem of the world? You can't! But you can make a big difference and if you learn to work with others so much more can be done.

Take It to God

Pray that God may show you what good things he would have you do. Pray for others to work with and learn to see the gifts in them and draw them out. You'll do the world so much more good in multiplying goodwill through others than by trying to accomplish everything by yourself.

Journal/Activity

Write down things that you can stop doing in your group and who else can do them. Encourage these people to help you and begin to let go and let them use their own gifts.

Make a Commitment that Lasts

My Life

How many times has a friend promised to meet you after a game and never shown up? Have you ever been stood up by a date? Did someone promise to help you study for a big test and not show? Can you identify with any of these situations? Are you guilty of any?

Setting the Scene

The Book of Numbers contains many foundational laws for the life of God's people. As God is faithful to his people so he calls his people.

Numbers 30:2-3

Reflection

You've heard the story about the boy who cried "wolf." Several times he cried "wolf" when there was no wolf. When one finally came and he called for help, no one would believe him. When people are known not to be faithful to their word, then you learn not to count on them.

If you build a reputation for letting others down, soon you won't be called on for help. If you're a person who wants to help others, then you have a major problem. Start all over proving you're trustworthy. Learn to make commitments you can keep and keep them. Know your limitations and then make promises that won't go beyond them. Soon people will learn to trust what you say and learn to depend on you.

Take It to God

Pray that God may teach you the importance of keeping your word. Pray that your commitment to following Christ and serving others may carry enough importance that you will keep that commitment as well.

Journal/Activity

Make a list of all your commitments. Are you able to carry out all of them well? If not, look at your list. Rank the commitments in order of importance to you. Begin at the bottom of your list and eliminate one thing. Check back later to see if you are able to perform what is left. If not, eliminate another item until you can fulfill all the commitments on your list.

_____

_____

_____

_____

_____

_____

_____

_____

_____

_____

_____

_____

_____

_____

_____

_____

_____

_____

You're Worth It!

Chapter VIII
Counting the Cost

Some time afterward, the word of the LORD came to Abram in a vision: Do not fear, Abram! I am your shield; I will make your reward very great ... Abram put his faith in the LORD, who attributed it to him as an act of righteousness. (Gn 15:1,6)

Depend on God

My Life

Do you know someone in your life who always keeps his/her promise? How does that affect your relationship with that person?

Setting the Scene

The Israelites are about to enter the Promised Land. Despite the countless times they failed to do God's will, God is still faithful. In this context He promises to be with them as they enter the Promised Land.

Deuteronomy 9:1-6

Reflection

Depend on God

A word spoken, a deed done,
a promise from his tongue,
like rain in due season
or the setting of the sun.
The tide that always rises
and subsides when its time comes
so God's word issues forth hope
that we learn to depend upon.
For when has God failed to fulfill
the promise that He gave?
Even when He was dead and buried
new life sprung forth from the grave.
In the beginning was the word
and the word shall always be
a surety to those who listen,
a foundation for those that believe.

In this passage God assures the Israelites that even though they are not faithful to him, he will give them the Promised Land. He made an oath and when God makes an oath, he keeps it.

Take It to God

What has God promised you? What has God done in your life? What has He already given you? What goals do you have for the future? What has God called you to do? Pray that in all your endeavors you will trust God for God has proven trustworthy. You can depend on God.

Journal/Activity

Place yourself as best you can in the place of one of the Israelites. Imagine all the doubts that would arise in so long a journey. Describe how you would feel once you entered the Promised Land.

Trust

My Life

Have you ever had a crush on someone? If you did, did you constantly look for signs of affection? If the person smiled and said "How are you?" would you be convinced that the feeling was mutual? Perhaps it didn't take much to give you hope. You would read the best into anything they would do or say. We always look for signs, proof that our convictions are true.

Setting the Scene

The Pharisees were among the Sanhedrin, the religious leaders of the Jewish people. They often are seen in Scripture as feeling threatened by Jesus and often challenged him with questions to try and disprove him.

Matthew 16:1-4

Reflection

The Pharisees were looking for a sign from Christ. I don't know what they needed. All you had to do was look at Jesus' life and listen to what he said. He told them no additional sign would be given but that of Jonah. He was referring to his own death and resurrection. What further proof do we ask of God?

We need that at times. We start to live for Jesus, doing good for others. We get a little frustrated because things don't work out the way we want them to or they don't work out quickly enough. We pray for something and then stand and watch looking for results. Is that faith?

We need to let go and trust God. Our will is not always God's will. When we pray we need to leave it with God. Looking for results only ties up our thoughts and stalls our ability to actively serve God and others. God has already given us all the hope we need. We have Jesus' death and resurrection. We have His promises. We have the actions of the Spirit in our own lives.

Take It to God

Pray that God will strengthen your faith. Learn to love without looking for results. We need to strive for unconditional love. Learn to find hope in the little signs already there, such as a smile or someone we care for saying "How are You?"

Journal/Activity

Imagine you have a friend who is really struggling in their faith in Christ. Write them a letter on why you think Christ's death and resurrection should give hope and a reason to trust God.

_____

_____

_____

_____

_____

_____

_____

_____

_____

_____

_____

_____

_____

_____

_____

_____

_____

Sensitivity

My Life

Have you tried to say the right thing but said it the wrong way? Instead of helping others you hurt them?

Setting the Scene

The Apostles preached the good news throughout Judea and the surrounding area. Their message was challenging. Some came to believe. Others were against their message. And others heard the words, but did not understand.

Acts 16:16-19

Reflection

Many times we fall into ruts in our relationships and react defensively the moment someone speaks to us. They'll begin to speak, and we'll react before they finish what they are saying. It may be because they have corrected us so often we put up a defensive wall to prevent another put down. It could be a coach who is constantly negative, a boss who never has anything good to say, or our parents. We could even do the same to our friends. At times it may be because of the *way* we say things and not *what* we say. Sometimes may because of a negative image we have of a person. We expect the worst. Regardless of our words, our negative attitude can come through because of the tone of our voice or attitude.

The girl in this passage is much the same. What she was saying was correct but Paul knew something was wrong. The spirit within her was not from God. Paul addressed her problem and, in Jesus' name, helped her.

Do you condemn people? Do you look at some of the things people do and decide whether they are good or evil? You don't have that right. God calls you to love. He calls you to be sensitive. He calls you to be aware of where people are coming from and to meet them on common ground.

Take it to God

Pray you will be led by God's Spirit and you will speak and serve in a spirit of love not condemnation.

Journal/Activity

Good intentions do not justify bad actions. Understanding those good intentions can sometimes help to change the bad actions to good. Make a list of your bad actions. What was the good you intended. What can you do to accomplish your good intentions without the bad actions.

God Will Give Us Words to Speak

My Life

In what situations do you find it most difficult to speak? Do you find it difficult because of a situation or because of the pressure you put on yourself?

Setting the Scene

Jesus is sending his disciples out to spread his Word. He knows that there are many that will not accept their message and so he warns them.

Matthew 10:16-20

Reflection

Funerals have to be among the most difficult occasions in which to find the words to say. When you go to the funeral home and see your bereaved friend or relative, you can't find the right words to say. Having been on both sides of that experience many times, I find the most important statement is not in your words but in your presence. When you are present to people in their time of need, you have already said that you care.

Learn to focus more on loving. In those instances that are most difficult, be at peace. You may be there more to listen than to speak. If you do speak, respond out of the love that you have for that person. God has promised to help us with words to speak. If your words come from the heart, they will be sufficient.

Take It to God

As you approach these difficult situations take time out to pray. Pray that God will give you peace and trust in him. Pray that if the time comes to speak that He will give you the words to say. Look for opportunities to love and know that the fact that you care enough to be there has already said a lot.

Journal/Activity

Visit someone who is lonely, a shut-in, someone at a nursing home, or a sick or elderly relative or neighbor. Be present to the person and learn to focus on their need and respond with love.

A Little Anger Can Be Good

My Life

What do you do with your feelings? You're often told to hold them in. Mom may yell at you but you're not supposed to yell back. A friend double-crosses you and you're not supposed to seek vengeance. Your teacher seems unfair, yet you must treat her with respect. Whether it's friendship, parents, elders, or dating, you always have to remain unemotional and hold the feelings in. If this is true, what are emotions there for and when are you supposed to use them? Aren't you ever supposed to get angry?

Setting the Scene

The money changers in the temple were there in order to serve a useful purpose. Jews came from all over the known world and needed to change their money into local currencies so they could purchase what they needed for the ritual sacrifices in the temple. Unfortunately, many money changers were not honest and cheated their customers.

Matthew 21:12-13

Reflection

All your feelings are indicators. They are there to help you identify positive or negative experiences. They are neither good nor evil. What you do with them can be either. Pain from sitting on a piece of glass isn't evil. It simply identifies a negative experience that you should know. Now you can complain about the pain but if you didn't have it you could bleed to death before you would do anything. In a sense the pain here is good. A pleasurable experience could be warm rays of sun on the beach. When you're there too long you start to become sunburned and it starts to hurt. If it didn't hurt, you might stay on the beach until you got third degree burns.

Here, in the temple, Jesus experiences the emotion of anger. It is neither good nor evil. It simply is. What he does with the feeling is what counts. In this case we see Jesus allowing his anger to spur him to action. It has its place under the right circumstances and when it is used for a good purpose.

When have you been angry? What did you do with the feelings? If you took action, were you in control? Was the intention of your action good?

Take It to God

Pray that God may help you to control your emotions, especially at the times when it is appropriate to act upon those feelings. Pray that your intent will be good and that the results will be constructive.

Journal/Activity

Go back to the experience of anger that you recalled. Write out a scenario in which you feel the same anger but record different ways you could use the anger for good and what the possible results would be.

Quality, Not Quantity

My Life

Have you ever felt alone with a just cause? You started out with support and then you find yourself wondering where everybody went? It's one thing to say you'll stand up for what you believe no matter what anyone says, it's another thing to do it.

Setting the Scene

Gideon was one of the judges in Israel. This was before they had kings or prophets. The judges served as tribal leaders. Here Gideon seeks to form a small army, inspiring them with the knowledge that God will give them victory.

Judges 7:2-7

Reflection

When I read this passage, I get an image of a lineup of soldiers before their commanding officer. The officer explains that he needs several volunteers for a dangerous mission behind enemy lines. Any soldier willing to risk his life should take one step forward. All at once the entire line takes one step back, except one man. The commanding officer congratulates the brave volunteer for his willingness to go it alone against incredible odds.

When we are trying to do good for our neighbor or for God, it may mean stepping out on our own, or almost on our own. Occasionally, when the water gets rough, our support can dwindle.

When Gideon was preparing for battle, I'm sure he felt his strength was in numbers. God saw differently. He knew that a few soldiers with true conviction were better than many with divided allegiance. Division among your friends can subvert the cause you're fighting for. So Gideon went with 300 into battle rather than the 22,000 that he had at the beginning. When the numbers of those who support you dwindle, don't give up. Those who remain with you will be those who really care. Whether it's supporting a friend who is in trouble or fighting for a just cause, it's not the numbers that count, but the heart of the few who remain.

You're Worth It!

Take It to God

Pray for true friends who share the same convictions. Pray that you may always be sure of God's presence in whatever task you undertake. Pray for those whose convictions are weak, that they may grow stronger in their love for God and others.

Journal/Activity

Watch the movie "Gandhi" and see the true story of how one man's peaceful resistance grew into a movement that freed a country from the rule of a foreign nation.

There Will Be Doubts

My Life

Have you ever made a decision to do something or found yourself in some circumstance where you wonder if you've done the right thing after all? Whether or not you feel certain of what you've done, you still might question God.

Setting the Scene

This is early in the story of the origins of God's people. They are not a people yet. Abraham here is known as Abram and is just now hearing God's call.

Genesis 15:1-6

Reflection

Abram is in a situation in which he has made a decision and now wonders what's next. He left his homeland to answer God's call, believing in God's promise of many descendants. The kind of questions going through his mind must be similar to the questions we have in the face of doubt. Did I make the right decision? Was it really God calling me? Can God fulfill his promise?

What questions have you asked yourself? Did you speak up to a friend who now isn't speaking to you? You wonder if you should have kept quiet. Are you in the midst of a new move and you wonder if you'll ever find a friend?

It could be holding your ground and not going with the popular opinion or standing up for someone who is being mistreated. Sometimes the price we pay causes us to wonder if we've made the right decision.

If your motives were good, nine times out of ten your decision was correct. In those instances where we have made a mistake, God will be there to help us. He granted Abram and his wife children in their old age and a home to call their own. He can help you make decisions and see you through to the fulfillment of your dreams.

Take It to God

When presented with moments of decision, pray for God's guidance and pray for faith in the Lord. Doubt has accompanied the journey of many of God's saints. Doubts will go with you, as well. When faced with doubt, turn to God, that he may help you to hold your ground and believe in your calling and follow the Lord.

Journal/Activity

Tonight go out and look at the stars in the sky and imagine what Abram was feeling when God told him how numerous his descendants would be.

The Source Can Come Through

My Life

Is there someone you can count on to help you no matter what? If you were facing a difficult situation and you knew they were coming, would you wait for them?

Setting the Scene

Jesus has died, risen and ascended into heaven. The Apostles have been challenged with spreading His Kingdom and they have been promised the Holy Spirit.

Acts 2:1-8

Reflection

In a close high school basketball game, you often look to your best player to pull you through. The score could be tied with no time left on the clock and your best player comes to the free throw line. He calmly bounces the ball a few times, looks up at the basket, and shoots. Swish, the ball slides through the rim and snaps the cord of the net. Once again, when the pressure's on, "Old Reliable" comes through.

The Apostles, in Chapter 2 of Acts, are found in Jerusalem waiting for the Holy Spirit and like the player you counted on in the basketball game, the Spirit comes through. Jesus had just ascended into heaven, and the apostles were left with the great commission of preaching about him to the world. How could they communicate with so many? Who would help with those from foreign countries? Who would believe their message?

What impossible situations have you been faced with? How did you work through the problem? After it was over was it really that bad?

Whether for explaining unapproved actions, speaking on another's behalf, or trying to convince others of another point of view, learn to turn to the Holy Spirit. The Spirit broke through communication barriers with the Apostles, the Spirit can also help you today.

Take It to God

Before every moment of confrontation or crisis ask God to prepare the hearts of others to be open and to give you the best words to say and the ability to live well the words you speak, in order to convince others of the message you bring.

Journal/Activity

Think back over your last week and consider the messages that God may have brought to you through others but you were not receptive to their word. What possible messages have you missed?

You're Worth It!

Chapter IX
Social Issues

Jesus replied, "The first is this: 'Hear, O Israel! The Lord our God is Lord alone! You shall love the Lord your God with all your heart, with all your soul, with all your mind, and with all your strength.' The second is this: 'You shall love your neighbor as yourself.' There is no other commandment greater than these. (Mk 12:29-31)

Turning the Cheek

My Life

Have you ever been wronged by someone else and in your anger you struck back? Does that kind of response always work?

Setting the Scene

In Luke's version of the Sermon on the Mount Jesus is speaking on a plain, but the style is still familiar. Jesus talks about the old law and challenges his people to take another step.

Luke 6:27-29

Reflection

Turning our cheek can be a powerful weapon against an aggressive, violent foe. The most significant cheek turning experience I have ever had was during my senior year in high school. Our school had its share of problems. Violence in our schools is nothing new. While standing at my locker a group of about ten young men came running by, apparently escaping from some trouble they had already been in. As they went by several of them struck me as they ran. None of them stopped. I wisely kept my back turned to them so no great harm was caused. I was thankful to God for not getting hurt and I probably threw up a quick prayer of help prior to their hitting me. Another group, about the same size, came running through the corridor. They also used me as a punching bag. This time they stopped and one of them held off and belted me quite hard on the back of my head. I turned around and told him he had a great right. They just stood there looking at me not saying a word. I asked them how they were doing and wished them a good day. After staring at me for a brief moment they took off.

The next day I saw the kid with the good right, bragging to a friend about his great punch. I walked up to him and asked him how he was, what was new and just basically tried to be friendly. For that brief minute, he stood there with his mouth hanging open about three inches. I finally said I had to get to class and off I went with a broad smile and the satisfaction of knowing the power of peace and turning one's cheek.

You're Worth It!

Take It to God

When have you been in a situation when you could have turned your cheek? Those types of situations are very difficult but they are a good opportunity to show God's love. As others put you down for what you believe or hurt you for no cause at all, pray that God may protect you and enable you to love that person.

Journal/Activity

Turning the cheek is not usually a physical thing, but the opportunity may come in a verbal dispute. Think back to the last argument you were in. Reconstruct the conversation and whenever you recall an abusive comment, return the comment with kindness and continue the conversation until its conclusion.

Reaching Out to the Poor

My Life

How often have you heard others blame the poor for being poor and use that as their excuse not to help?

Setting the Scene

This psalm captures a theme common in many psalms and in the prophets. God has a special spot in his heart for the poor and he calls us to respond.

Psalm 41:1-4

Reflection

Do you see anything in this passage criticizing people who are poor? Is there any tone of judgment insinuating that these people are simply lazy and won't work? How many times have you heard others or yourself show disregard for the poor rather than compassion? I've heard it before; "They don't want to work. They'd rather be on welfare. They have so many kids so they can collect more money." I didn't know we knew the hearts of others. Maybe someone should talk to the psalmist and straighten him out or maybe we need to listen to God's Word and stop judging our neighbor.

It's not for us to decide who is deserving of our love. Being poor often carries with it a low self-esteem and a sense of hopelessness. What the poor need is love and a sense of hope that they can work out of their poverty. Nobody wants their children to go hungry. No one wants to be without shelter or the means to improve themselves. The greatest motivation, if the motivation is what is needed, is love. When you do something for which you are praised, you feel good about yourself and what you have done. Your self-regard is high because of the regard others have shown you.

How can you reach out to the poor? Does the Church have programs to feed and clothe people?

Take It to God

Pray that you may see the image of God in these people for they are created in God's image. Pray for compassion for the poor. It's not a request from God, but one of the basic requirements of being a Christian.

Journal/Activity

Contact your church and find out what you can do or who you can contact. Ask your church for materials on poverty so you can better understand their plight.

Even Israel Needed Correction

My Life

Have you ever heard: "The Church should stay out of politics. Why can't our priest talk about God? What is this social justice stuff?" So go the complaints of those of us comfortable Christians who wish that those who speak against our social problems would leave well enough alone.

Setting the Scene

Isaiah was one of the major prophets of the Old Testament. He was constantly calling God's people back to compassion for the poor. He cried out against the political leaders of his day. Many wanted the prophet to be silent and leave politics alone. He was sharing God's Word.

Isaiah 31:1-3

Reflection

To those who wish that priests or ministers would mind their own business, it might be good to look at the prophet Isaiah and see what their business is in the first place.

This passage and others in Scripture suggest that we have a responsibility to address the moral actions of our governments. Isaiah cried out against his Israelite countrymen in order that they might not fear their enemy because of their military strength, but turn to God. The point of Isaiah's argument here, when put into modern terminology and in a modern context, would sound similar to the cries against the arms race of the 1970s and 1980s or maybe the recent trend toward the death penalty.

I leave it for you to pray over particular issues and decide according to your conscience. Know, though, that it is the place of the Church to search the Scriptures and Tradition and give us guidance regarding social justice and moral issues. It is our calling to stand up as the prophet Isaiah and speak up for the oppressed.

Take It to God

In general, know that it is the calling of God's messengers, with whom Christians should be aligned, to speak up when the rights of others are abused, whether by a person or a government. Pray for openness to criticism of your government's moral misgivings and your role in calling attention to the mistakes for which we all take responsibility.

Journal/Activity

Think of an issue in the area of political or social immorality about which the Church has spoken and which you have been silent about or have disagreed. Ask someone for material on the subject to read or for an agency that you can contact that may help you to see the concern of the Church.

_____

_____

_____

_____

_____

_____

_____

_____

_____

_____

_____

_____

_____

_____

_____

_____

The Call of Love

My Life

Have you ever tried to comprehend the magnitude of the universe? It is so vast that we can't comprehend it. Can the same be said for the creation of God made in his image?

Setting the Scene

Jesus is confronted by another member of the Sanhedrin, a scribe. He asked him a sincere question after noticing Jesus' wisdom.

Mark 12:29-31

Reflection

What is your whole heart? Consider the person you love more than any other and the time in which you felt the strongest human compassion for that person. If that isn't the greatest expression of the feeling of your heart, then reach beyond it. Love God with your whole heart.

When have you held the deepest sense of wonder? When have you felt most in touch with yourself? In the depth of your whole being be present to God. The soul, to the Hebrew mind, from whom this commandment finds its expression, was the culmination of all that we are. Love God with your whole being.

What provokes more thought in you than any other moment? Reach beyond the depth of that thought and contemplate who God is. Do you picture God as you can best understand him and all that he has done? Love God with all your mind.

When have you been pushed to the limits of your emotional, physical, and mental strength? Sense the feeling of extension of your whole being. With all the strength you have, love God.

How do you love yourself? You feed yourself when in any form of need you seek to have your need met. It does not matter what effort you must take. You love yourself. Love others in the same manner.

Take It to God

This love, in all its depth, toward God and your neighbor, is the foundation of personal growth and fulfillment, and Christian discipleship. More than anything else for which you pray, pray that God may increase the depth of love you have for the Lord, for others, and for yourself.

Journal/Activity

Do something kind for a person that you find difficult to love.

_____

_____

_____

_____

_____

_____

_____

_____

_____

_____

_____

_____

_____

_____

_____

_____

_____

_____

_____

Color-Blind Faith

My Life

Do you open yourself to all who come to you?

Setting the Scene

The first Christians were Jews who recognized Jesus as their Messiah. They had to come to realize that God's invitation knew no limits. They had to come to realize their own prejudices.

Acts 10:34-35

Reflection

It's been several years since the movie "Guess Who's Coming to Dinner?" has graced the big screen, but the message is still needed today. It was the story of a white woman coming home with her fiancé to meet her parents. To their surprise he was a black man. The story line dealt with the prejudice of the couple's parents and its effect on accepting their love for each other. The story ends with the stubborn father realizing that love knows no racial boundaries.

Segregation is a result of prejudice. It excludes some people from others based on criteria which is genetically inherent to a group of people. Verse 35 of this passage clearly states that segregation has no home in the Church. You must read all of chapter 10 to see how God reveals this truth to both Peter and Cornelius. The conclusion is that God receives all who accept him.

Do you have friends of other races? If so, are you comfortable being with them when your other friends are around? If you are asked out for a date by someone of another race, does their racial difference enter in to your decision? Do acts of segregation and prejudice against any group of people upset you?

Take It to God

Know that your discomforts with others based on color of skin is a distinct sign of prejudice. Pray that as God increases your love for others and decreases your prejudice, your tendencies to show favoritism will decrease. Pray for a willingness to break down racially motivated segregation where you find it. Pray for the courage to hold your ground when others come against you because of the stand you take.

Journal/Activity

Read the book "Black Like Me" or watch the movie. This true story will help you to see the folly of our prejudices toward one another.

_____

_____

_____

_____

_____

_____

_____

_____

_____

_____

_____

_____

_____

_____

_____

_____

_____

_____

_____

_____

Christian Unity

My Life

Have you ever had people judge you because of what church you go to or by the way you dress?

Setting the Scene

As Paul concludes his letter to the Romans he speaks of how we must live for Christ and in doing that we cannot judge others.

Romans 14:4-7

Reflection

I've been introduced to people by fellow Christians as Catholic, but they love me anyway. I've helped people find Christ who later came back to help me get saved because I'm Catholic. Over and over again I've seen signs of division between Christians based on religious prejudice. At times it angers me and other times I just smile and shake my head. It's not their fault. They were taught what they believe by their church leaders and it will take time and patience for them to realize that their denomination isn't the only Christian church.

There are differences between denominations. We don't all understand the Scriptures the same. We may place emphasis on different passages, and the experience of past prejudices has caused us to see our differences rather than the faith in Jesus we share in common. No arguments of religious differences will bring us together but only a fellowship which emphasizes what we share in common.

Do you look down on a particular church? Why? Is your church perfect? Do you look down on those within your church because of differences?

Take It to God

Ask God to help you break down divisions between brothers and sisters in Christ. Jesus prayed that we would be one as he and the Father are one. Pray for unity and love in the church that images the unity and love between Jesus and his Father. Pray that your own religious prejudice would be replaced with an acceptance of other Christians.

Journal/Activity

Pick a Christian church with which you are uncomfortable and visit during a Sunday service. Afterward, note similarities between that church and your church.

The Call of Christian Witness

My Life

Who are the people in your life that are poor, bound by addiction, blind to other people's goodness? How do you reach out to them?

Setting the Scene

Jesus begins his public ministry in Luke's Gospel with the reading from the prophet Isaiah. As you may remember Isaiah was a prophet who spoke out for justice. In his prophecies concerning the Messiah he spoke of him who came for the poor. Jesus announces that he is that Messiah.

Luke 4:16-19

Reflection

Who were the poor? Who were the captives and the prisoners? Who were the blind of which Jesus spoke and how did he give them sight? What was the Good News He shared and how was that prophecy fulfilled in Him?

In the Beatitudes, Jesus began by promising the reign of God to the poor in spirit. To some extent we are all poor, blind, and imprisoned. We've been bound by our own selfish desires, blind to a life of love, poor in a spiritual wealth that he offers to all of us. We know that in Jesus the spiritual wealth, freedom, and vision is ours. We are not only called to tap into the Spirit ourselves but to share it with others, to announce a year of favor from the Lord.

Free from blinding prejudices, reach out to anyone who will receive your love.

Rich with God's Spirit, through your relationship with Christ, share his love with anyone you know who is lonely or hurt.

As you can now see more clearly why you are here and the vision of life you've experienced, give others hope when they're depressed. Help others see the reason to follow Christ.

Take It to God

In all your friendships, in all your activities concerning social justice, be a witness for Christ. Don't go to change anyone. Go and share the Good News and allow Christ to do the changing. Don't try and play savior, just tell others about the one we already have. Show them His love by loving others as He has loved. Pray for the continued freedom, vision, and richness in Spirit that you need to be the person God calls you to be.

Journal/Activity

Read a book on the life of Mother Teresa. As you read about this modern-day saint, consider how she acquired her spirit, her vision, and her freedom.

Love Begins at Home

My Life

What are our traditions? What are the excuses we use for not loving those that are closest to us? Why the Pharisees would dispense with God's Word for their own traditions is not important. The important thing is why do we?

Setting the Scene

Again Jesus is confronted by the Pharisees. He is questioned about the Apostles not following their ritual practices.

Matthew 15:1-6

Reflection

Jesus response to the Pharisees was to call them to task for not taking care of their parents while they run around pretending to be so righteous. It isn't easy. Your home is the best training ground for Christian discipleship that you have. When loving others, there is less risk because there isn't as much of a relationship at stake. At home you're known, weaknesses and all. You are more vulnerable. The words we speak carry more meaning for all the masks are buried. When you love your family on a regular basis – Mom, Dad, brothers, and sisters – you will have the capability to love your neighbor. We are talking about actions and not feelings.

Examine your relationship with each member of your family. Keeping in mind the lessons on social justice, prejudice, and loving your friends, What can you apply to your relationship with them?

With regard to justice, are you fair with each member of your family? Do you expect more from them than you give? Do you give expecting no favors?

With respect to prejudice, do you anticipate what they're going to say? Do you assume the worst without giving them a chance?

With regard to loving your neighbor, are the standards of love you have for your family the same as you have for others?

Take It to God

Pray that in the most difficult battleground for spiritual growth and Christian witness that you may have, you may be able to love your neighbor when your neighbor is your own family.

Journal/Activity

Choose the member of your family with whom you have the greatest difficulty getting along and record your answers to the questions above. During the next week focus on treating them with justice without prejudice and with love.

_____

_____

_____

_____

_____

_____

_____

_____

_____

_____

_____

_____

_____

_____

_____

_____

You're Worth It!

Chapter X
Getting Back To God

We know that all things work for good for those who love God, who are called according to his purpose. For those he foreknew he also predestined to be conformed to the image of his Son, so that he might be the first-born among many brothers. And those he predestined he also called; and those he called he also justified; and those he justified he also glorified. (Rom 8:28-30)

Don't Straddle the Fence

My Life

Have you ever reached a point in your life where you have to make a choice which way you're going to go? What forks in the road have you come to where you have to make such a choice?

Setting the Scene

In the first few chapters of Revelation, seven churches with different issues are addressed. Some have been very faithful to God while others have not been faithful.

Revelation 3:15-20

Reflection

Fence-straddling, not hot, not cold, but trying to live in both worlds. Claim to be a Christian, go to church, to youth groups, even pray a little, then go out and get drunk, put people down, and live selfishly. We want to live in both worlds without one affecting the other. Have God's forgiveness and the warmth of Christian community on one hand and the best of the life that does not live for God and others. We can portray an image of a Church that is full of compromise. By our example many are disillusioned and some leave the church because they'll look at a congregation and see an unchristian community. Get off the fence! If you fall off you'll just hurt yourself and others. Make a decision for Jesus. You need to choose if you truly want to believe and follow.

That's basically the message to the Church in Laodicea. In verse 20, Jesus stands at the door of our heart ready to come in as Lord. He has to be number one in our lives. With Him as the director, our play can only have a happy ending even if there are trials along the way. Without Him our life will never have meaning or fulfillment. What areas of your life do you need to give up? Alcohol, drugs, sexual immorality, dishonesty, or things that promote or lead to that kind of activity? That's where the fence border is. If we're on the fence then we have one foot in that world. Take it out and place both feet firmly on the path to life.

Take It to God

Pray that you will not be distracted from living totally for Him.

Journal/Activity

Draw a picket fence. On each board write an area of your life where you compromise your relationship with God. Write also the situations in which you place yourself that make it difficult to follow Jesus. This is often where the decision to straddle the fence comes from. The actions of compromise only naturally flow from positions of compromise. This fence separates you from a close relationship with God. It needs to be taken down one board at a time.

He's as Near as My Heart

My Life

Have you ever gone looking for something and you just couldn't find it? When you finally do find it are you surprised that it was right under your nose all the time?

Setting the Scene

Back to Paul's letter to the Romans. He has already spoken to them about sin, salvation, and life in God's Spirit, and here he talks about what we need to do to receive all that God offers.

Romans 10:6-13

Reflection

He's As Near As My Heart

An emptiness within
loneliness, no sense of being,
I have longed to have purpose,
I long to be free.
Grudgingly I wonder
finding in nature's grace
beauty for which to behold,
but where the glance of His gently face?
I was told He'd be here
where they found their sense of being,
but for me, my quest unanswered,
where can the answer be?
I lay back, tired upon my bed,
resting my weary frame
gently within, a calling,
He calls me forth by name.
Always there within me,
there my answer be.
He's as near as my heart
waiting to set me free.

We hear of others who have gone on a retreat at a lake and found Christ. They had a mountaintop experience and dog gone it, it was on a mountain. You can't take the lake or the mountain with you. To have what they found, you don't need to go to a mountain or a lake. In the quiet of your own room or in the midst of Christian friends Jesus waits for you. He's as close as your heart and your opening of your heart to him. Whenever you are in search of God don't look any further than where you are. He's as near as your heart.

Take It to God & Journal/Activity

Sometimes it is the clutter of a busy life that causes us not to take notice of God in our heart. Take a quiet walk or just be in a place alone. Open your heart to God. Be quiet and be present to the Holy Spirit. Promise your life to God.

_____

_____

_____

_____

_____

_____

_____

_____

_____

_____

_____

_____

_____

_____

Believe in Him Who Loves You

My Life

Think of a time when you realized how much someone loved you. What was it that made you realize that they cared?

Setting the Scene

John's Gospel used very different imagery than the other gospels. John uses images of light, water, and rebirth to try and help Nicodemus understand God's love and the new life God offers.

John 3:16-21

Reflection

Fire and brimstone just wasn't Jesus' style and it shouldn't be ours today. The preacher who threatens hell just doesn't find a home in Jesus' words here. The prospect of not being with God forever is our decision, not his. God honors our decision, He doesn't make it. Jesus' attitude is one of acceptance, but then what other attitude would he have in light of what he has done for us and the motivation that moved him?

First, let's look at the Father. How many of us would give up the One who means more to us than anything for someone else and then not care about the One for whom we made the sacrifice? It doesn't make sense. That's what God did for us. He gave up His only begotten Son, Jesus, for our offenses. He allowed His Son to suffer as a sign of His love. After that, why would He pull back on His love for us? If He loved us that much to begin with, He will continue to stand by us.

In the case of Jesus, he was willing to make the ultimate sacrifice of his life for us. You don't just lay your life down for someone else and not care what happens to them. After such a sacrifice who could care more than Jesus?

That is our God. That is what is waiting for us. With the level of sacrifice that has been made, what is so great that we could ever have done that Jesus hasn't already satisfied? Whatever the punishment you may feel you deserve for anything you have done, Jesus has accepted it for you. He has paid the price.

You're Worth It!

Take It to God

He now waits for you to simply accept His love for you and to love Him in return. In order to love Him He simply asks you to love and follow Him. As you pray today, pray that you will accept God's love for you expressed on the cross. Let that love be your motivation for following Him.

Journal/Activity

Remember the picket fence you made? In order to follow Christ look back at the boards on the fence and make a decision to change some of the circumstances of your life so you can follow Christ.

_____

_____

_____

_____

_____

_____

_____

_____

_____

_____

_____

_____

_____

_____

_____

_____

How Is God Trying to Get Your Attention?

My Life

Think of a time when you were very aware of God in your life.

Setting the Scene

Moses was in exile from Egypt. He was a Jewish boy raised in the Pharaoh's home. He had killed an Egyptian in defending a Hebrew slave from harm. God now calls Moses to go and set the Hebrew people free.

Exodus 3:1-5

Reflection

There was little question in Moses' mind that God was calling him. It isn't quite as obvious for us because a burning bush isn't an everyday medium for the voice of God. Still, throughout our lives, God does call us. Where are some of the places where you have sensed God?

If I were to break down the occasions in which I am most aware of God's presence I would use three categories: people in whom I see God, places that remind me of Him, or an experience of Him. The three of these together paint the picture of the community gathered sharing the Sacraments of God.

Think of the people you know who remind you of Jesus. What about them reminds you of Jesus? Through their actions what may God be teaching you about living the Christian life? Spend some time with these people and ask them questions which will enable them to share with you those things that will help you follow Christ.

What places remind you of God? What about that place reminds you of the Lord? If it is an experience, what does the experience show you about God? Sometimes it is not an experience, but the beauty of a place that reminds us of our creator. How often do you take time out for these special places?

Different experiences in our life, good or bad, cause us to turn to God. Negative experiences cause me to seek help while positive experiences cause me to be grateful. In such experiences do you think of God?

Throughout our lives there will be people, places, and things through which God can teach us or try to get our attention. Do we seek to find Him through these everyday occurrences?

Take It to God

Pray for an awareness of God's presence through both everyday and unusual occurrences. Reflect on what you can learn from experiences as they come along and allow them to help you draw closer to God.

Journal/Activity

In place of the picket fence it is now time to build a foundation for a life in Christ. Using a cement block foundation, place in each block the name of an experience, place, or person in which you see God. This is the beginning of your new foundation.

_____

_____

_____

_____

_____

_____

_____

_____

_____

_____

_____

_____

_____

Humbling Ourselves in Order to Rise

My Life

Think of the most incredible sacrifice you have ever seen someone make for another person. How do you think the benefactor of that sacrifice felt?

Setting the Scene

This passage is known to be the earliest recorded hymn of the Christian community. It was probably sung in the earliest liturgies and contains the core belief of the early Christians.

Philippians 2:6-11

Reflection

When I was in grade school, I saw a film in religion class about a vineyard owner. On the property there were ants, black and red, who were constantly fighting. The vineyard owner, through his concern for the ants well-being, asked his son to become one of them to communicate his concern. The camera work was incredible as they effectively portrayed, through the activity of these ants, the story of Christ becoming a man, including the ants killing the son of the vineyard owner in his ant farm.

What constantly runs through my mind, as I reflect on this story is the sacrifice the young man made in becoming an ant. There's just no way I could give up being human to become an ant. The experience must have been so humbling. Yet even more humbling than becoming an ant, is God becoming a man. This movie brought that home to me so clearly.

Try and imagine what Jesus must have given up for us. Try to picture heaven and all the power and honor he had. That's what this passage is all about. Jesus gave up all that for us and then rose to greater honor.

Paul asks us to have that same attitude. What are you willing to give up in order to become all you can be? To what extent are you willing to understand another's experience in order to be of service to them? Will you humble yourself and consider the needs of others first?

Take It to God

This is the mind of Christ of which Paul speaks. Pray that Jesus will enable you to be humble. Pray for a willingness to admit where you are wrong. Be willing to sacrifice now for what you can be for others.

Journal/Activity

Take five to ten minutes and just watch a colony of ants or some goldfish. Consider what it would be like to be one of them. What would you give up not to be human? Consider all that you would give up and then consider how much more Jesus gave up for you.

Jesus' Prayer for Us

My Life

When something critical emerges in your life, who do you ask to pray for you? Is it the most religious people you know?

Setting the Scene

This is John's version of Jesus' final prayer before he is arrested and faces death.

John 17:20-23

Reflection

For some reason, we believe the prayers of the holiest people we know will be answered before ours, after all they're so close to God. If we continue in that line of thought, a prayer spoken by Jesus himself would have to carry a special delivery stamp to the Father. The value of this prayer for me is in the circumstances in which He prayed and that for which He prayed.

This prayer, in John's Gospel, appears just before Jesus arrest. In a moment like this, how many of us would be praying for somebody else? The beauty of this portion of the prayer is that he is praying for us — future Christians. To think of others, especially those yet to come, is so unselfish under these circumstances. It attests to the depth of Jesus' love. What he prayed for strikes home even more, when you consider where we are today.

Jesus prayed for a unity of love among believers. How many denominations of Christians are there and what is our attitude toward each other? Some people won't date someone because the person doesn't go to their church. People will act like they are better than someone else because of their religious beliefs. The church we go to does carry importance, but what good is it if we don't love one another?

Take It to God

Jesus prayed for Christian unity. If that's his prayer then it should be ours. Pray that you may begin to develop a whole new attitude toward your fellow Christians. Appreciate your differences and share what you have in common. Don't try and convert each other. Seek to be one in Spirit and the Spirit, over time, will lead us the rest of the way.

Journal/Activity

Go to the head of your youth ministry or your pastor. Ask him or her to arrange for your group to do something with a group from another denomination of Christians. It can be social, service, spiritual, or a combination.

_____

_____

_____

_____

_____

_____

_____

_____

_____

_____

_____

_____

_____

_____

_____

_____

_____

_____

Who Do I Say He Is?

My Life

What images come to mind as you try to picture Jesus and your relationship with him?

Setting the Scene

Jesus and his Apostles had been in ministry together for quite some time. After all the preaching, miracles, and love Jesus wants to know if they understand who he is. Peter answers.

Matthew 16:13-17

Reflection

Who do you say that Jesus is? If you say a friend that's good. What is a friend to you? To me a friend is someone who will always be there for me. A friend doesn't desert me when I'm down, but is there to help me up. A friend isn't always able to help though and my friends have faults as well, so a friend Jesus is but so much more as well.

The people of his day said he was a prophet. A prophet tells us how we can follow God. He speaks up when we are wrong and affirms us when we are right. Jesus certainly was a prophet. He showed us the way to God yet He was more. He did more than tell us the way.

Peter said He was the Messiah, the Son of God. The Messiah was He who came to save the people, the Anointed One. He more than shows us the way, He is the Way. He's more than just a friend, He is the greatest of friends. He's more than another man. He is the Son of God. Is that what Jesus is to you?

We have looked at both the humanity and divinity of Jesus. We know what He did for us and how He loves us. As God's Son and the one who meets our needs, He is Lord. Lord means He is number one in our life. For Peter, He was.

Take It to God

How high on your list is Jesus? As you pray today, consider those you love most and seek to place Jesus high on that list. Make him number one in your life. As your Lord, He can enable you to love others.

You're Worth It!

It is not easy, but neither was the cross for Jesus. Who will you say that He is?

Journal/Activity

Have a friend hide something in a park. Have them go along with you but not give you any guidance as to where it is or possibly even what it is. They can console you and give you encouragement (prophet and friend). After a while they can then guide you to the hidden object. Reflect on the difference between Jesus as Lord and friend.

What Does It Mean to Believe?

My Life

Think of a time when you were totally frustrated because things didn't go the way you wanted them to go. How did you respond?

Setting the Scene

This letter was written to a small community of disciples that was under persecution. They were in need of encouragement to remain strong in their faith.

Hebrews 11:1-3

Reflection

To me, the true measure of our faith in God is more evident when things don't go as we planned rather than when they do. It's at this time that the conviction for things we do not see really counts. Can I trust God when his will isn't mine? When you think about it, can you trust a God whose will is always yours? I couldn't. I want a God who is greater than me, who sees what I can't see and knows what I don't know. If He didn't then He wouldn't be God. I believe in a God that is greater than me, so things don't have to go my way in order for me to believe. I still have hopes. I still experience disappointments. It is my faith that helps me through those times.

What are your hopes? Are the desires of the heart good or are they selfish? If they are selfish then do you believe God will try to fulfill those desires or help you to change? What circumstances have you had where your hope seemed diminished? Did you learn anything about faith? Did you learn anything about yourself and your relationship with God?

Take It to God

Pray, as you read, for a strengthening of your faith and a hope that will never diminish. Give to God those areas of your life where you feel the greatest need.

Journal/Activity

If you read through this chapter, you will find that the writer used many examples of people of faith. He shows how God fulfilled their hopes. With many people it took a very long time, but their faith sustained them. Read through this chapter and let their faith be an inspiration to you.

_____

_____

_____

_____

_____

_____

_____

_____

_____

_____

_____

_____

_____

_____

_____

_____

_____

_____

_____

_____

Evidence of Jesus in Me

My Life

Think of a person that you see as a holy example of being a Christian. How would you describe that person to someone else?

Setting the Scene

Paul is encouraging the Galatian community to reject a life that is contrary to Christ and live a life in God's Spirit. He then explains the characteristics that are evident in a Christian.

Galatians 5:22-26

Reflection

There are many signs of Jesus growing in each of us. The signs may vary according to what our need may be. Gradually change comes. It may be good to sit down with another Christian who knows you and share the growth you've seen after six months or more. My first experience of this helped me to appreciate God's working in my life. We don't always see the change that others see.

We were nearing the end of my senior year in high school in our campaigners group. Campaigners was a fellowship group in Young Life for those seeking to develop their commitment to Christ. We were paired off to share with each other how we've seen ourselves grow. I was paired with one of the leaders. I shared with him how God had helped me to control my tongue. It had been months since I cussed or swore. He laughed and told me about an experience he had had with me.

It was a couple days after I came home from camp. I was walking home from work and he was riding his bike on the street where I was crossing. He stopped to ask me if I had a good time at camp. I can't repeat exactly what I said, but I can tell you it was colorful. In so many words I said that I had a good time and he was right in guessing that I did.

Here we were nine months later laughing at my former habits, yet appreciating the change. If you took an hour to watch a five year old, you wouldn't see much growth. If you came back a year later, you would notice a significant change.

Take It to God

Growth takes time, but gradually, as you seek real change in your life, the fruit of God's Spirit will help you grow from within. Select virtues mentioned in this passage in which you are weakest. Pray that God may help you to grow in these areas. Each time a circumstance arises where you are tested, know that this is a time for growth and pray for God's help.

Journal/Activity

Sit down with a close Christian friend and ask them to share with you how he/she has seen you grow in the past year. From here consider where you need to grow during the coming year. Be patient.

God, My Closest Friend

My Life

How do you feel about your time with God? Do you get to church as late as possible and leave as early as you can? How much time do you spend with God outside of church? Would you describe your relationship as a friend?

Setting the Scene

In this passage Moses seeks God's assurance of his presence as they continue their journey to the Promised Land.

Exodus 33:12-17

Reflection

As you read this passage do you sense that Moses did what he did because of his religious beliefs? I don't. I sense that he did what God asked of him because he loved God and had a relationship with him that provoked a desire to serve. This is the essence of the entire Scriptures. Our relationship with God is the key to our ability to love, to be what we are created to be. It's not how religious you appear to be or how proper you complete religious duties. Do you know God? Is God your intimate friend? If he is, then you want to pray. You want to go to church. Singing songs is not a major problem because each song is a prayer. Why are we in such a hurry to leave this community fellowship with our intimate friend, God? Maybe it's because for so many of us, we haven't allowed our friendship with God to become intimate.

Take It to God

God seeks to have a friendship with us that is meaningful. In your time with God place your emphasis on friendship and not fulfilling a religious duty. Spend time with Him and enjoy His company, for God is our closest friend. Pray that your friendship with God will grow.

Journal/Activity

Write down the characteristics of a close friendship. Next to each

write how this characteristic is present between you and God. Determine what you need to do to get closer to God.

_____

_____

_____

_____

_____

_____

_____

_____

_____

_____

_____

_____

_____

_____

_____

_____

_____

_____

_____

_____

_____

_____

Standing Strong in Christ

My Life

Think of the equipment that a football player wears. How does each piece of equipment help him to perform as a football player?

Setting the Scene

As Paul concludes his letter to the Ephesians he gives some final words of instruction for Christian households. He concludes with a final word of encouragement for all of them and some words of prayer.

Ephesians 6:10-17

Reflection

This passage, through its imagery, details for us how we draw our strength from the Lord, in order that we may be able to resist temptation and remain loyal to him. Breaking down the imagery we are left with truth, justice, zeal, peace, faith, salvation, and the Word of God.

Truth enables us not to be deceived. We do belong to God and are made in his image We don't have to listen to those who tell us otherwise.

Justice – Jesus died for us. There is nothing for which we aren't forgiven. Likewise, we must also forgive others. In doing this we build bridges of healing and love.

Zeal carries us through the struggles and the resistance of those who don't see the goodness in Christ. Our enthusiasm and positive attitude can rub off on others, helping them to have hope.

Peace is a contentment within our own spirit, knowing our worth and being happy with who we are. We bring that inner peace to others. We can't bring peace to others unless we have peace within ourselves.

Faith – no matter what happens, we know that God is with us and believe that he will enable us to win our spiritual battles.

Salvation – that we are becoming all that we were meant to be. We aren't losers. We are the image of God and he isn't a loser.

Through the word of God, Jesus, all was created and all returns to him. If we know his word we will have an understanding of all the other gifts mentioned. It is our guide to life.

You're Worth It!

Take It to God

Whether your struggles are personal or with friends, at school or at home, in all your struggles, rely on Christ. Ask Him, in each situation, how these gifts will enable you to do your best. Stress your knowledge of His Word for in His Word will you gain understanding of the rest. Pray for God to increase your strength in those gifts where you are weak.

Journal/Activity

Draw a picture of a person wearing armor as depicted in this passage. For each of the various attributes draw that part in proportion to how strong that characteristic is for you. If your faith is weak then your shield will be the size of a thimble. After you are done look at your armor to determine how prepared you are to do battle against evil in your life. What do you need to work on?

_____

_____

_____

_____

_____

_____

_____

_____

_____

_____

_____

_____

_____

Standing Together You and I

My Life

Have you ever been by yourself standing up for a just cause? Have you ever been in a similar situation but with someone who shares your convictions? When do you feel more confident?

Setting the Scene

Matthew's Gospel contains several passages that emphasize the value of the Christian community. In this passage the community plays an important role in correcting others. Here the emphasis is on communal prayer.

Matthew 18:19-20

Reflection

This passage helps us stand strong in Christ and develop those gifts which help us to do what is important. Just as important is the recognition of the special presence between Christians in prayer together. We build each other up, making strong the gifts we each possess.

When you go through an entire day at school with little reinforcement for your Christian values, the armor of God that you wear gets tarnished. Daily reinforcement through prayer is great, but you need to know you're not alone in this army. What army has its members fight alone? We learn to join together so we can be strong. My three closest friends and my brother all made commitments to Christ the same summer. The combination of my prayer times alone and my fellowship with them enabled me to grow in Christ and not give in to being less than I could be. Are those you spend time with committed to following Christ? If so, how much time do you spend sharing Christ, your struggles, and prayer?

If you don't have close Christian friends, seek to find them. We Christians need each other. We who do have each other must learn the importance of prayer together. We seem almost afraid of it, but if we build our relationships on Christ, we will have so much love to share with one another that we didn't realize was there.

Take It to God

Pray for a friend with whom you can share prayer together. Experience the special presence of God when two or more of you gather in his name.

Journal/Activity

Ask at least one or more close friends to pray with you once a week. You may even decide to read the same Scriptures and share with each other. This gutsy step is absolutely essential for Christian growth. If you are dating than ask that person to join you. If you can't ask them then go back and reflect on the portion of this devotional on dating.

How Will I Make It?

My Life

Have you ever found yourself in a situation where you just weren't prepared for the task? Kind of like showing up for a test having studied the wrong chapter. You might have the right stuff but you studied in the wrong place.

Setting the Scene

This is one of many parables Jesus used to help us understand his message about the Kingdom of God. Parables were analogies using the things in peoples' everyday lives to help them understand his message.

Luke 8:1-15

Reflection

We've all heard the parable of the sower of the seed. The farmer spreads the seed, seeds of faith to all who receive it. The seed is the same for all of us, but its growth is different. How do you know whether your seed will grow? It's up to you. What kind of soil are you?

The rocky or footpath ground is the person who may have had a great retreat experience or heard that Jesus was the answer to everything, so decided to follow Jesus. That person didn't give thought to any sacrifice or change in lifestyle. An emotional experience or an escape from responsibility was the foundation. When the emotions subsided or the person found that life's responsibilities were still there, they gave up not ever making a true commitment to Jesus. What kind of thought have you given to following Christ? Have you counted the cost? You still can.

The briars and the thorns represent the person who had a very real experience of faith, but constantly was torn between Christ and the other concerns of life. With the onslaught of popularity, drug abuse, alcohol abuse, the constant allure of sex, and all this compounded by peer pressure that calls us to conformity, this person becomes choked up and rejects Christ through constant compromise. The need to belong can also be met through fellowship with other Christian teens. It's a matter of recognizing the impact of those things which influence our lives.

The fertile ground is the person who considers what it means to follow Christ, counts the cost, and says *yes* to Jesus. In following up on that decision, they make sure the soil was good by ridding themselves of the weeds in their life. What remains that distracts you from being Christian and causes you to dwell in temptation?

Take it to God

Pray for a stronger conviction of love for Jesus. Pray that in your conviction you may have the discipline to remain in situations that encourage your growth. Keep in fellowship with other Christians and keep your attention focused on Christ. Continue to live a life of loving others and you will be fertile soil.

Journal/Activity

Weed a garden. Everytime you pull a weed think of something in your life that you need to pull out or it will choke your spiritual growth. Then cultivate and water the soil so that what is left will grow. What do you need to nurture so that you will grow?

We Will Make It!

My Life

In certain situations, do you wonder if things are going to turn out all right? What if the worst possible thing has happened and you don't know what to do?

Setting the Scene

Paul has just assured us of God's presence in our lives and his promise to help us in our weakness even as we pray. He then continues with these words of hope. If you have time read through to the end of the chapter.

Romans 8:28-31

Reflection

When I entered college, my dream was to teach religion full time at a local Catholic high school. After four years, my dream was realized. Everything fell into place so beautifully. I actually started on the staff midway through my senior year in college. I taught the next year as well. Everything was going better than expected. I loved teaching and I felt much ground was being broken in helping teens find Christ. I even had students who didn't have me as a teacher coming to see me before or after school to talk about their problems and their relationship with God.

Near the end of my second year I was called in to the principal's office and informed that my contract would not be renewed. I can't tell you how stunned I was. That afternoon, while at home, a friend called. She asked me how I was doing and I responded with the beginning of this passage, Romans 8:28. "We know that all things work for good for those who love God." She knew then that something must be wrong. That's not how I usually answer "How are you?"

I was reminding myself of a basic truth. You remember the passage on the armor of God? I was using it here. I was reminding myself of my faith with the truth of God's Word. I got a job in a factory right away and made a lot of money, but bending steel wasn't the same as teaching. I thought about my students more than my work for the first few months.

Through the help of prayer, Scripture, and friends, I soon learned to act on Romans 8:28. I decided this was where God wanted me. In the two years I was there, I was involved in starting two prayer groups and a third one was started by the time I started my new career as a youth minister.

As I look back, losing that job opened up a new life in which I could help so many more people. I love youth ministry and the opportunities it gives me to meet the needs of youth and give youth the opportunity to serve others. I enjoyed the new setting that I was in and the relationships I was able to build with teens in parish ministry.

Take It to God

There is no other way to explain how Romans 8:28 applies to one's life than to say that if your love for God remains constant, good will come out of your life. It may take time, but it's worth it. In the meantime, ask God to help you to trust God in all circumstances.

Journal/Activity

Sit down with an older Christian and share this passage. Ask them to share with you how God has made things work together for the good in their lives.

You're Worth It!

My Life

Why are you God's buried treasure, his pearl of great price?

Setting the Scene

We began with this parable and we conclude with it. Parables were Jesus' way of using everyday examples to help us understand his message. You may not own a pearl or discover a buried treasure, but as you read this passage understand that Jesus was trying to capture a sense of the greatest possible worth with those images.

Matthew 13:44-46

Reflection

God's reign is a ruling of the heart as he brings back into order the creation he made. Of all his creations, the one God treasures most is you and me. We are the ones God made in his image. We are the ones for whom God sent his Son to die, that a new life could be possible, a life in which the image of God will be restored to us. The key is what lies within. Is the reign of God at hand within you?

Your life is a series of relationships through which you learn to love. Each relationship prepares you for the next and all relationships prepare you for your ultimate relationship with God. Through this devotional we have looked at the struggles you have with parents, family, friends, and your neighbor. We've looked at how God can help you as you submit yourself to the Lord. As God works within your heart and you seek to follow the guidelines to life He has given you, the buried treasure, for which the Lord gave up everything, emerges.

You are that valuable pearl and the beauty that lies within can only be brought forth by God. You can't always change your circumstances, and you can't change others, but you can become all that God created you to be. When that happens, circumstances can improve and your relationships with others, more times than not, will also improve.

Take It to God

Pray for Jesus to truly be in charge of your life, with the number one purpose of drawing out of you your buried treasure. That buried treasure is you, the person whom Christ looked down upon and considered worth the sacrifice of his life. He decided, You're Worth It!

Journal/Activity

Review your journal entries form this devotional. What steps for spiritual growth do you need to take? List them and dedicate yourself to them with all your heart. It will take effort but remember, you're worth it!!

Notes

You're Worth It!

Notes

Notes

You're Worth It!

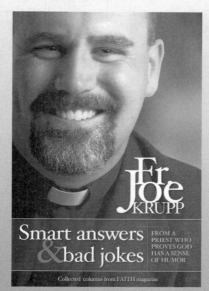

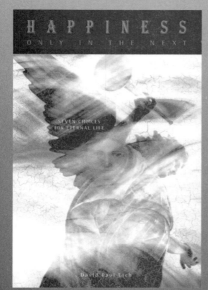
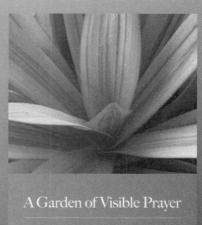